ILLINOIS POLITICS
CORRUPTION, SELFISHNESS, GREED

I0425099

ILLINOIS POLITICS
CORRUPTION, SELFISHNESS, GREED

Dr. Charles W Zamzow Jr

Published
2009

© 2009 Charles Zamzow. Printed and bound in the United States of America All Rights reserved. No part of this book may he reproduced or transmitted in any form or by any means, electronic or mechanical, including photocopying, recording, or by an information storage and retrieval system—except by a reviewer who may quote brief passages in a review to be printed in a magazine or newspaper—without permission in writing from the publisher, or information, please contact Jupiter Technical Solutions, PO Box 335, Ottawa, IL. 61350.

Although the author and publisher have made every effort to ensure the accuracy and completeness of information contained in this book, we assume no responsibility for errors, inaccuracies, omissions, or any inconsistency herein. Any slights of people, places, or organizations are unintentional.

ATTENTION CORPORATIONS, UNIVERSITIES, COLLEGES, AND PROFESSIONAL ORGANIZATIONS;
Quantity discounts are available on bulk purchases of this book for educational purposes Special books or book excerpts can also be created to the specific needs. For information, please contact Jupiter Technical Solutions, PO Box 335, Ottawa, IL. 61350

Dedicated to the millions of honest hard working families that are struggling each and every day to make ends meet. Families that are teaching their children to be honest and treat people with respect.

"Power does not corrupt men. Fools, however, if they get into a position of power, corrupt power."
—*George Bernard Shaw*

Contents

Illinois has long legacy of public corruption
At least 79 elected officials have been convicted of
wrongdoing since 1972

Two powerful forces keep stoking the fires of corruption:
selfishness **and **greed.*

Cost of corruption by state officials high for Illinois taxpayers

Prevention: An Effective Tool to Reduce Corruption in the
Illinois Government

Corruption Symposium: A Case Study on 'The Chicago Way'

Prevention Is the Only Solution to Corruption

List of Illustrations

ABOUT THE AUTHOR

Charlie has lived in the midwest for 20 years. He has traveled the better part of his life in the construction, engineering, and maintenance industries. His education includes a Bachelors, Juris doctor, and a PhD. He has taught college as a adjunct instructor and is very interested in politics. This is his first shot at some investigative journalism in the area of political corruption. His other books he has published are more related to the reengineering of business processes. He hopes folks that purchase this book will like what he has put together.

Other Books:
Business Process Reengineering
7 Critical Success Factors for a Smooth Transformation of Your Organization Process
ISBN: 978-1-6048-1326-5
Published By WordClay
www.wordclay.com

POLITICAL CORRUPTION IN ILLINOIS
AN INFAMOUS PAST

We are the Land of Lincoln. But the last half of the 20th century in Illinois politics has been dominated by names and phrases less frequently associated with great virtue and noble causes.

Orville Hodge, state auditor of public accounts, was convicted in 1956 of embezzling$2 million in state funds.

Paul Powell, secretary of state, stashed $900,000 cash in shoeboxes in his hotel room; they were discovered after his death in 1970.

Otto Kerner, governor, was convicted in 1972 on income tax charges involving stock in racetracks acquired while in office.

Cement Bribery, a former state senate president, three other legislators, and a lobbyist were convicted in 1975 of a scheme to influence legislation regulating truck hauling.

Richard J. Daley, mayor of Chicago, presided over the legendary political machine in Chicago and Cook County from 1955 until his death in 1976.

Operation Greylord, a federal investigation into the Chicago court system, was completed in 1988with convictions and guilty pleas from 87 court personnel and attorneys, including 13 judges.

William J. Scott, Illinois attorney general, was convicted in 1991 of income tax charges involving misuse of campaign funds.

Operation Silver Shovel, a federal investigation into corruption in Chicago city government, ended in 1996 with 18 convictions and guilty pleas from public employees and six aldermen.

Daniel Rostenkowski, congressman and chairman of the House Ways and Means Committee, was convicted in 1996 of mail fraud charges related to public corruption.

Management Services of Illinois, its two principal officers, and two Illinois Department of Public Aid officials were convicted of fraud and bribery in 1998 after a federal investigation into that agency's awarded contracts.

A SCANDALOUS PRESENT

The turn of a new century has not ushered in a new era of clean politics in Illinois. Rather, political corruption has continued with al vengeance in all its traditional forms: influence peddling, political patronage, bribes, extortion, fraud, misappropriation of funds, and vote fraud.

Operation Safe Road, a federal investigation into former Governor George Ryan's eight-year tenure as secretary of state resulted in the 2003conviction of his campaign fund and his chief of staff on federal racketeering charges. George Ryan was indicted in 2004. At the end of 2005, there had been 73 convictions or guilty pleas as a result of the investigation and George Ryan's trial was still in progress.

Hired Truck Scandal, a federal investigation into corruption in a public program in Chicago, resulted in 37 indictments and 26 guilty pleasing 2005. The investigation broadened into an investigation of hiring practices by the city of Chicago.

East St. Louis Vote Fraud Scandal, a federal investigation into vote fraud and public corruption in the city of East St. Louis, ended in 2005 with the conviction of one current and one former city official and seven precinct workers. In December, a former city police chief was convicted on political corruption and tax fraud.

Other 2005 Highlights included the resignation of a state legislator after being convicted of election fraud; the indictment of the chief of staff to a former House speaker on public corruption charges; the indictment of a board member of a state pension fund and the conviction of two representative of investment firms for a kickback scheme; the ongoing federal investigations into the awarding of contracts by the Illinois State Toll Highway Authority and the hiring practices in the office of the governor and two state agencies.

THE EARLY YEARS

Illinois has long legacy of public corruption
At least 79 elected officials have been convicted of
wrongdoing since 1972

The Politics of Chicago have been dominated by controversy, corruption, turn-of-the-19th century businessmen, Irish Catholics, and Richard J. Daley and the Daley family. Democrats have usually dominated city politics, and they produced presidential nominees in Stephen Douglas (1860), Adlai Stevenson (1952 and 1956), and Barack Obama, who was nominated and elected in 2008.

19th century

In 1855, Chicago Mayor Levi Boone threw Chicago politics into the national spotlight with some interesting proposals that would lead to the Lager Beer Riot. During much of the last half of the 19th century, Chicago's politics were dominated by a growing Democratic Party organization dominated by ethnic ward-heelers. During the 1880s and 1890s, Chicago also had a powerful radical tradition with large and highly organized socialist, anarchist and labor organizations.

The politics of Chicago came into play after the Great Chicago Fire of 1871. For political reasons, a rumor was spread that a cow knocked over a lantern, thereby causing the fire. The election that year turned the fire into a *"political football"*, with controversy erupting over that was culpable for the fire's rapid and insufficiently controlled spread. The winning party used allegations of mismanagement to spread fear, causing some voters to vote more than once. This may have popularized the famous saying "vote early and often."

Chicago municipal politics began after European Americans defeated the last resistance of Native Americans in the Black Hawk War of 1832. The following year, Chicago received its first incorporation charter from the state legislature. Through the Civil War, as Chicago's white settlers struggled to establish a city on the western edge of the "frontier," Chicago politics was a contest between private interests and public needs. Money was needed to build an urban infrastructure of streets and sidewalks, sewer and water systems, schools and shops. Capital investment had to be found to support new commercial activities to create jobs and guarantee economic growth. But Chicago had only a property tax with which to finance such activities, and its residents were not eager to pay from their own pockets. Individuals exploited scarce public funds, as when in 1837 it was discovered that the Cook County School Commissioner had loaned the school fund, gathered through sale of federally donated land, to private real-estate speculators who defaulted on the loans, leaving the city without sufficient funds to operate the schools. Chicago residents who wanted federal government aid for infrastructure projects were thwarted by others who preferred private development. This contest in Chicago reflected a national conflict between the political parties over whether there was a public need for federal government to foster development that should supersede private interests. Until the Civil War era, private interests largely prevailed.

An uneasy relationship to the state of Illinois also characterized early Chicago politics. U.S. cities receive powers of government from their states. State law regulates the relationship between cities and counties and the relationship of a city to other municipal authorities such as school boards, and it confers and limits a city's powers to tax and to finance municipal development. Historically, there has been a power struggle within the state. In 1839, the state legislature abolished the office of high constable for Chicago and did not inform the city for two months. Some Chicagoans sarcastically replied that they hoped to be informed more quickly should the legislature decide "to remove Chicago from the shore of Lake Michigan."

By the 1850s, growing social divisions in the city gradually inserted ethnic rivalry into Chicago politics. In 1855, older residents tried to regulate the leisure activities of the newer communities of German and Irish immigrants by having the municipal government raise the cost of liquor licenses and require Sunday closing of saloons. The resulting Lager Beer Riot forced the government to rescind its efforts, and henceforth the city's immigrant groups demanded a voice in municipal politics previously dominated by a small group of men who had governed the city in their interests.

Dinner with Mayor Edward J. Kelly, 1938

The growing polarization within the Democratic and Republican parties along class and ethnic lines, along with an ongoing struggle between the city and the state over how much power Chicago should have to govern itself, characterized Chicago politics from the 1870s to the 1930s. These two elements fed upon each other as the city grew into an industrial metropolis and outpaced the legal restraints imposed by state law. The new state constitution of 1870 cancelled single-city charters, and in 1872 the legislature passed a Cities and Villages Act to apply to all incorporated areas with a population of 2,000 or more. This law suited the state's small homogeneous towns more than an industrial metropolis. From the early twentieth century, Chicago attempted to secure relief through a legislative grant of home rule powers. But every such effort was thwarted by the historical distrust between city and state and distrust of Chicagoans for one another. Fearing Chicago's growing influence in the state, the legislature carefully restricted the city's home rule powers, refused to allow consolidation of the city and Cook County governments, and from 1900 until the 1940s limited Chicago's representation in the legislature by refusing to fulfill its legal obligation to redistrict the state. Home rule efforts also foundered because they revived the ethnic and class conflict that had sparked political unrest in Chicago before the Civil War and that resurfaced when a group of prominent men attempted to control all relief and rebuilding in the city after the fire of 1871. Chicago workers accused these men of trying to control municipal government. These events, along with the street riots during the great railroad strike of 1877, the fears engendered by the Haymarket massacre of 1886, and the pressures of massive immigration, divided Chicagoans even more along class and ethnic lines, and they perceived home rule as a question of "who ruled at home." Chicago politics then became a struggle among various groups in the city to control municipal government for their advantage.

The political struggle taking place in Chicago from the 1870s until the 1930s reflected the struggle within the United States to redefine the nature and purposes of democratic government. Rural Midwesterners, African Americans from the South, and increasing numbers of Mexicans joined hundreds of thousands of European immigrants coming to Chicago seeking economic, political, and social opportunity. The poet Carl Sandburg celebrated Chicago's growth into the "City of the Big Shoulders" and "Hog Butcher for the World, Tool Maker, Stacker of Wheat, Player with Railroads and the Nation's Freight Handler." Others saw Chicago as the symbol of everything wrong with industrial capitalism. Englishman William Stead declared that "If Christ Came to Chicago" he would weep at what he saw, and to Upton Sinclair, Chicago was a "jungle" of human misery and exploitation

20th century

Worker exploitation, extremes of wealth and poverty, and the corruption of both businessmen and politicians all existed in Chicago because neither federal nor local governments had the power to confront the worst aspects of economic and social injustices that were multiplying in the nation's cities. In the absence of such power, Chicago's political parties functioned as machines that promised to deliver favors in return for votes. Often these favors went to the immigrant poor who needed help finding a job or feeding the family, but these favors also went to businessmen who received potentially lucrative contracts from the city council. The parties were also machines for enriching the politicians, as in the 1890s when the notorious aldermanic ring of "Gray Wolves" sold municipal contracts and franchises to build street railways, haul garbage, or lay gas mains to the highest bidders.

Public outrage over such actions, as well as the exposés by writers such as Stead and Sinclair, produced a "progressive" reform movement in Chicago, but there was never any agreement about the desired ends of such reform. Business and professional men, supported by the Republican Party, stressed that all municipal reform should bring expertise and fiscal efficiency into government. They unsuccessfully supported the home rule charter of 1907, opposed municipal ownership and control of public utilities, sought business control of the public schools, and wanted to exploit the economic possibilities of the lakefront. They demanded an end to patronage politics, the election of professional experts rather than party politicians to public office, and a strong-mayor system that would weaken the power of the city council. The city's ethnic and immigrant groups, generally supported by the Democratic Party, opposed many of these ideas, arguing that they were designed to deliver city government into the hands of middle-class businessmen.

Chicago's laborers, for example, sought municipal ownership as a way to control public resources. Ethnic voters supported a strong, ward-based city council as more democratic than a strong-mayor system. Unions opposed businessmen's ideas for the schools because they wanted school decisions kept closer to the people, but they also feared that business control of the school board would diminish the power the labor unions already wielded in school management.

Thousands of Chicago women worked through partisan political women's organizations, voluntary civic groups such as the Woman's City Club, and working women's organizations such as the Women's Trade Union League for progressive reforms to make the municipal government more responsive to the everyday needs of Chicago residents. These women called for putting public need ahead of private or even group interests. They demanded that the city provide more affordable housing, give teachers a greater voice in school decisions, provide a cleaner and more healthful urban environment—by building public beaches, preserving the lakefront for recreation, and instituting municipal ownership of garbage collection, for example—and pass new ordinances for fire prevention.

The political parties became the means for determining the outcome of the struggle over these issues, but not until the 1930s did the Democratic Party assume control of the city. Workingmen's parties and the Socialist Party attracted workers in the 1880s and 1890s. A small Labor Party ran candidates in the municipal elections of 1919. Progressive-minded men and women split from the regular Republicans to join the Progressive Party in 1912. Moreover, factional rivalry divided each party, and every municipal election was first a contest over who would control each party and then a contest among the parties to determine who would run the city. But the Democratic Party undercut all attempts to build a workers' party through patronage, promises to govern the city to the benefit of immigrants and the working class, and an alliance with the Chicago Federation of Labor. At the same time, the Republican Party became increasingly the party of the middle class and business and professional men. The city's African American residents, whose men were guaranteed the franchise after ratification of the Fifteenth Amendment in 1870, bucked this trend. They joined the party of Lincoln and secured election to a small number of countywide and state offices, elected their first alderman in 1915, and sent representatives to Congress on the Republican ticket. Chicago women did not fit neatly into Chicago party politics. Neither Democrats nor Republicans made any serious overtures to securing the party loyalty of women, who, despite gaining municipal suffrage in 1913, remained largely excluded from Chicago politics. The parties refused to nominate women for municipal offices and male voters largely refused to vote for any woman who stood as candidate. Chicago women practiced party politics, but they were much more likely than men in the decades immediately following woman suffrage to vote for the candidate rather than the party and especially to vote for any woman running for municipal office. Women also failed to control any important appointed municipal offices. When Mayor Thompson's commissioner of public welfare was forced to resign in 1916, the post remained vacant until the mayoral administration of William Dever (1923–1927). This was a particularly galling political defeat for women who had prized the creation of this office to address the problems of the city's neediest people. No woman was elected to the city council until 1971, when Marylou Hedlund and Anna Langford secured seats, and Jane Byrne (1979–1983) is the only woman ever elected mayor.

The ascendancy of the Democratic Party was not secured until Anton Cermak built a broad coalition of ethnic and working-class voters that secured his election to mayor in 1931. The Republican Party had meanwhile self-destructed, as progressive and liberal Republicans grew disgusted with the party's support of three-time mayor William Hale

Thompson, whom they regarded as a practitioner of blatant ethnic politics. His campaigns of 1915, 1919, and 1927 included crude ethnic baiting and a willingness to switch sides on any issue when it suited his purpose. Thompson's 1931 renomination for mayor by party leaders was the last straw for Republican luminaries such as Charles Merriam, Julius Rosenwald, Jane Addams, and Louise DeKoven Bowen. They, and other liberal Republicans, threw their support to Cermak, who's ethnic and anti-Prohibition credentials also recaptured working-class and ethnic voters who had drifted into the Thompson camp when he championed ethnic interests and opposed Prohibition. This attraction to Thompson and the Democratic Party's support for labor issues and anti-Prohibition stance had helped guarantee that a Labor Party never took hold. The Democratic Kelly-Nash machine of the 1930s finished Cermak's work. It brought Chicago unions securely into its orbit and encouraged the city's African American voters to abandon a Republican Party that more and more was a party of the white middle and upper classes. No Republican has been elected mayor since 1931, and few Republicans have even made it into the city council.

The New Deal of the 1930s and the Great Society of the 1960s gave the Democratic Party access to new funds and programs for housing, slum clearance, urban renewal, and education, through which to dispense patronage and maintain control of the city. Mayor Richard J. Daley (1955–1976) also kept the city and party financially sound by exploiting the state's refusal earlier in the century to consolidate the city and county governments or to give the city more control over municipal services such as the public schools. Cook County, for example, remained responsible for providing and funding many social services and maintaining the only public hospitals so that the city has never had to bear their financial burden. Although the mayor appointed the Board of Education, the school system was independent of the municipal government and its funding kept separate from the municipal budget. This structure meant that the mayor's office could simultaneously exert influence on the schools and disavow any political responsibility for managing or funding the system. Mayor Harold Washington (1983–1987) used it to claim he had no responsibility for trying to settle the month-long teachers' strike that pushed back the opening of the 1987 school year by four weeks.

Mayor Daley and the Democrats also controlled Chicago politics by exploiting growing racial and class antagonisms. From the 1940s, growing African American and Hispanic populations competed for jobs, housing, and schools. Middle-class whites fled to the suburbs and the Democrats retained the support of ethnic, working-class whites by allowing de facto social and economic segregation in neighborhoods, housing, jobs, and schools. The selection of loyal black politicians for municipal posts that might provide jobs but offered little power kept African American voters loyal to the Democratic Party well into the 1970s. To make Chicago the "city that works," Daley courted the business community through contracts on new public works projects—much as the city council had done earlier in the century. He structured favorable real-estate and taxation arrangements and an urban renewal program that benefited the middle class and businessmen more than the urban poor.

As Chicago moved toward the end of the twentieth century, the brief surge of African American power embodied in Harold Washington's two elections ebbed, and Richard M. Daley was elected mayor. Chicago politics changed under the second Mayor Daley. He has maintained Harold Washington's initiatives in making Chicago politics and governance more inclusive as to race and gender and has fine-tuned the first Mayor Daley's idea of making the city's economic development its first priority. Yet, the exposés of sweetheart deals and contracts doled out to friends and supporters of the Democratic Party suggest that patronage politics is enough of a way of life in Chicago that it will never die.

The political environment in Chicago in the 1910s and 1920s let organized crime flourish to the point that many Chicago policemen earned more money from pay-offs than from the city. This same culture led directly to the Chicago Black Sox scandal of game fixing by the Chicago White Sox in 1919.

The modern era of politics is still dominated by machine politics in many ways, and the Chicago Democratic Machine became a style honed and perfected by Richard J. Daley after his election in 1955. Further evidence of this is the fact that his son, Richard M. Daley, is the current mayor.

Richard J. Daley's mastery of machine politics preserved the Chicago Democratic Machine long after the demise of similar machines in other large American cities. During much of that time, the city administration found opposition mainly from a liberal "independent" faction of the Democratic Party. This included African Americans and Latinos. In the Lakeview/Uptown 46th Ward. The first Latino to announce an aldermanic bid against a Daley loyalist was Jose (Cha-Cha) Jimenez, the Young Lords founder. The independents finally won control of city government in 1983 with the election of Harold Washington. Since Washington's death, Chicago has returned to the leadership of the Democratic organization led by Richard M. Daley, although it may differ from the previous ward-based organization, as it relies on other groups, such as the Hispanic Democratic Organization.

A point of interest is the party leanings of the city. For much of the last century, Chicago has been considered one of the largest Democratic strongholds in the United States. For example, the citizens of Chicago have not elected a Republican mayor since 1927, when William Thompson was voted into office. Today, only one city council member is Republican.

The police corruption that came to the light from the Summerdale Scandal of 1960, where police officers kept stolen property or sold it and kept the cash, was another black eye on the local political scene of Chicago.

The Daley faction, with financial help from Joseph P. Kennedy, Sr., helped elect John F. Kennedy to the office of President of the United States in the 1960 presidential election. The electoral votes from the state of Illinois, with nearly half its population located in Chicago-dominated Cook County, were a deciding factor in the win for Kennedy over Richard Nixon.

Chicago politics have also hosted some much publicized campaigns and conventions. The Democratic Party decided on Harry S. Truman as the vice-presidential candidate at the 1944 Democratic National Convention. The 1968 Democratic National Convention was the scene of mass political rallies and discontent, leading to the famous trial of the Chicago Seven.

Home-town columnist Mike Royko wrote satirically that Chicago's motto (*Urbs in Horto* or "City in a Garden") should instead be *Ubi Ist Mio*, or "Where's Mine?"

21st century

In 2008 Governor Rod Blagojevich was arrested on charges of trying to sell the vacant United States Senate seat of President Barack Obama. He was impeached and removed from office by the state legislature in Jan. 2009. Blagojevich will also face a criminal trial in federal court.

Public corruption has been an unfortunate aspect of Illinois politics for a century and a half. Even before Governor Blagojevich tried to sell the vacant senate seat to the highest bidder, the people of the state were exposed continuously to outrageous corruption scandals.

The state history of political corruption features Paul Powell, a former secretary of state, who died leaving hundreds of thousands of dollars hoarded in shoeboxes in his closet, 13 judges nabbed in Operation Greylord for fixing court cases, and a state auditor who embezzled more than $1.5 million in state funds and bought two planes, four cars, and two homes with the money.

Since 1972 there have been three governors before Governor Blagojevich, state legislators, two congressmen, 19 Cook County judges, 30 Aldermen, and other statewide officials convicted of corruption. Altogether there have been 1,000 public officials and businessmen convicted of public corruption since 1970.

The history of public corruption in Illinois goes as far back as 1860s when the state's largest city, Chicago, was growing rapidly and with much disorder which provided ample opportunities for corruption. This time period is characterized by several corruption cases in the city including a city council ring of aldermen on the take known as McCauley's Nineteen, and county commissioners involved in a City Hall painting contract scandal. Of the 14 aldermen and public official indicted in that scandal four were convicted and several others lost their reelection bids in the elections of 1871.

At the same time, a gambling kingpin, Michael Cassius McDonald, created Chicago's political machine. Public officials were handing out contracts, jobs and social services in exchange for political support. McDonald is credited with "electing aldermen who lorded it in the city council and county commissioners who stole everything in sight and for providing contracts for public works that had thievery written between the lines."

Machine politics and corruption have been directly linked ever since the late 1860s following the civil war and the Great Chicago Fire.

Serving Time

The ranks of imprisoned poles include three former Illinois governors — George Ryan, Dan Walker and Otto Kerner Jr.

Ryan, a rare Republican in the heavily Democratic state and Gov. Rod Blagojevich's predecessor, is serving a six-year prison sentence after being convicted in April 2006 on racketeering and fraud charges. A decade-long investigation began with the sale of driver's licenses for bribes and led to the conviction of dozens of people who worked for Ryan when he was secretary of state and governor.

The probe began when federal investigators looking into a deadly crash in Wisconsin that killed six children uncovered a scheme in Ryan's secretary of state office in which unqualified truck drivers has obtained licenses through bribes. As the Associated Press reported upon his conviction: "The probe expanded over the next eight years into a wide-ranging corruption investigation that eventually reached Ryan in the governor's office."

Walker's crimes were committed after he served as governor from 1973 to 1977. The Democrat and World War II and Korean War veteran was convicted of fraud related to his stewardship of the First American Savings & Loan Association of Oak Brook. News reports at the time indicated that he received more than $1 million in fraudulent loans for his business and repairs on his yacht, the "Governor's Lady." The federal government later bailed out the bankrupt S&L and Walker served 18 months of a seven-year sentence in federal prison.

Kerner, a Democrat who was governor from 1961 to 1968 and later served as a judge on the U.S. Court of Appeals, was found guilty in 1973 of bribery, conspiracy, perjury and related charges for taking payoffs from a racetrack operator in exchange for choice racing dates and two expressway exits to funnel fans to the horse races.

The scandal erupted because Marge Lindheimer Everett, manager of Arlington Park and Washington Park racetracks, deducted the value of the stock she gave on her federal income tax returns under her own theory that bribery was an ordinary and necessary business expense in Illinois.

After resigning his judgeship, Kerner was sentenced to three years in federal prison and fined $50,000.

A history of graft

Chicago, with its long history as a center of vice and organized crime, has had its share of official graft.
One of the most notorious alleged recipients was never convicted of any crime.

William "Big Bill" Thompson, who served as mayor from 1915 to 1923 and again from 1927 to 1931, was the last Republican to serve as mayor of the "City of Broad Shoulders." He returned to office the second time with the support of gangster Al Capone, pledging to clean up organized crime in the city but instead targeting reformers. Upon his defeat in 1931 the Chicago Tribune leveled the harshest accusations against Thompson in an editorial:
"For Chicago Thompson has meant filth, corruption, obscenity, idiocy and bankruptcy," the newspaper said. ".... He has given the city an international reputation for moronic buffoonery, barbaric crime, triumphant hoodlumism, unchecked graft, and a dejected citizenship. ... He made Chicago a byword for the collapse of American civilization."

Upon his death, two safe-deposit boxes in his name containing nearly $1.5 million in cash reportedly were discovered.

The Daley legacy

Investigations of possible mayoral misbehavior have been commonplace in recent years.

Current Mayor Richard Daley's administration has been investigated for corruption. In a federal probe that is ongoing, Robert Sorich, Daley's patronage chief, was convicted in 2006 for rewarding the mayor's political allies with city jobs and promotions. Daley has not been accused of wrongdoing.

His father, the late Mayor Richard J. Daley, built the once-mighty machine that doled out jobs and favors in exchange for support for Democrats on Election Day. He was never charged with criminal wrongdoing, but several of his high-ranking aides were sent to prison for political patronage.

Other state officials have apparently prospered from their positions of public trust without ever facing trial. A large cache of cash surfaced in 1971, shortly after the death of Illinois Secretary of State Paul Powell, who served 30 years as a state legislator before assuming his final post.

Governor Accused in Scheme to Sell Obama's Senate Seat

The governor of Illinois brazenly put up for sale his appointment of Barack Obama's successor in the United States Senate, federal prosecutors said Tuesday. In recorded conversations with advisers, the governor, Rod R. Blagojevich, seemed alternately boastful, flip and spiteful about the Senate choice, which he crassly likened at one point to that of a sports agent shopping around a free agent for the steepest price, a federal affidavit showed. At times, he even weighed aloud appointing himself to the job, the prosecutors said.

"I've got this thing," Mr. Blagojevich said on one recording, according to the affidavit, "and it's [expletive] golden. And I'm just not giving it up for [expletive] anything. I'm not going to do it. And I can always use it. I can parachute me there."

Mr. Blagojevich (pronounced bluh-GOY-uh-vich), a Democrat, was arrested at his home at dawn Tuesday on charges of conspiracy and soliciting bribes. A lawyer for the governor said he denied any wrongdoing.

The corruption case extended well beyond the Senate appointment, stunned even a state that thought it had seen every brand of political corruption, created grave doubt over how or when President-elect Obama's successor in the Senate might now be selected, and left many wondering who else might yet be implicated in Mr. Blagojevich's brash negotiations, which were captured in phone calls recorded by federal agents since before Election Day.

"The conduct would make Lincoln roll over in his grave," Patrick J. Fitzgerald, the United States attorney for the Northern District of Illinois, said in announcing the arrest of Mr. Blagojevich and his chief of staff, John Harris.

Under state law, Mr. Blagojevich is assigned to name a replacement for Mr. Obama, who recently resigned as Illinois' junior senator with two years remaining in his term.

Mr. Obama, who Mr. Fitzgerald said was not implicated in the case, sought to put distance between himself and the governor during brief remarks on Tuesday afternoon and later in an interview with The Chicago Tribune, saying he did not discuss his Senate seat with Mr. Blagojevich.

"I had no contact with the governor or his office, and so we were not — I was not aware of what was happening," Mr. Obama said. "And as I said, it's a sad day for Illinois. Beyond that, I don't think it's appropriate to comment."

Throughout his career, Mr. Obama has adroitly straddled the state's bruising politics, forming alliances with some old-style politicians even as he pressed for ethics reform. But Mr. Obama had long been estranged from the governor, even though some in his political circle have had relationships with both of them, including Rahm Emanuel, his chief of staff, and Emil Jones Jr., the retiring State Senate president and a longtime mentor.

The federal accusations against Mr. Blagojevich go beyond the Senate question into what the authorities here described as a "political corruption crime spree."

The governor is accused of racing to solicit millions of dollars in donations from people with state business before an ethics law bars such behavior in January, and threatening to rescind state money this fall from businesses, including a

Chicago hospital for children, whose executives refused to give him money. He is also accused of putting pressure on The Chicago Tribune to fire members of its editorial board who had criticized him or lose the governor's help on the possible sale of Wrigley Field, which is owned by the Tribune Company and is home to the Chicago Cubs.

Mr. Blagojevich, who looked somber during an afternoon appearance in federal court, was released from custody on a $4,500 recognizance bond after surrendering his passport. A hearing in federal court will be held in January to determine whether there is probable cause to go forward with the charges.

Sheldon Sorosky, his lawyer, later told reporters that the governor was "very surprised and certainly feels that he did not do anything wrong."

According to the affidavit, in more than a month of recorded phone calls at his home and campaign office, Mr. Blagojevich considered numerous ways that he might personally and politically gain from the various Senate candidates, none of whom were identified by name in the court filing. One possible choice might be able to help him secure a post with the new administration as secretary of health and human services or energy; a "three way" deal involving a union and a candidate might win him a union leadership post; or perhaps, he could secure the high-paying helm of a nonprofit organization that could be created for him.

Mr. Blagojevich, whose administration has for years been known to be the subject of a federal corruption investigation, also spoke of his family's financial woes and said he had three criteria for selecting the new senator: "Our legal situation, our personal situation, my political situation — this decision, like every other one, needs to be based on that."

In several possible situations, the affidavit says, Mr. Blagojevich seemed to refer to plans already under way to make money or win a job (for him or his wife, Patti) in exchange for a particular Senate selection, raising the specter that there might be others, including some of the Senate candidates, who were participating or at least considering participating in such deals.

Even before Mr. Obama was elected president, Mr. Blagojevich was recorded telling an adviser on Oct. 31 that he was giving greater consideration to one candidate (described only as Senate Candidate 5) after an approach by "an associate" of that candidate who offered to raise $500,000 for Mr. Blagojevich, while another emissary of the Senate hopeful offered to raise $1 million. "We were approached 'pay to play,' " Mr. Blagojevich said on a recording. But prosecutors, who have made it clear that the investigation is continuing and who issued a plea on Tuesday for people to come forward with information, warned against drawing any conclusions about the true roles of candidates or anyone else in Mr. Blagojevich's plans. And they emphasized repeatedly that the affidavit made "no allegations against the president-elect whatsoever."

Several people among the half-dozen whose names have been suggested publicly as Senate possibilities did not respond to requests for interviews. Others, including Representative Jesse L. Jackson Jr. and Mr. Jones of the State Senate, who has been one of Mr. Blagojevich's few allies in Springfield, issued statements expressing shock over the accusations, but they did not answer requests for interviews.

"If these allegations are proved true, I am outraged by the appalling, pay-to-play schemes hatched at the highest levels of our state government," said Mr. Jackson, who had openly expressed interest in Mr. Obama's old job and who met with Mr. Blagojevich, whom he is not known to be close to, for 90 minutes on Monday afternoon to discuss the post. In November, Mr. Blagojevich asserted to an adviser, the affidavit says, that he knew whom Mr. Obama wanted named as his successor — described in the affidavit as Senate Candidate 1, a reference apparently to Valerie Jarrett, a senior adviser to Mr. Obama — but cursed him in apparent frustration that "they're not willing to give me anything except appreciation."

Ms. Jarrett later took her name out of consideration for the post. But at one point, Mr. Blagojevich spoke to an official at the Service Employees International Union, the affidavit says, with the "understanding that the union official was an emissary" to discuss the possibility of a "three-way deal" that would put Ms. Jarrett in the Senate seat, Mr. Blagojevich at the leadership of Change to Win, a union-affiliated group, and "in exchange, the president-elect could help Change to Win with its legislative agenda."

Officials at the service union said they had no reason to believe that any union officials were involved in wrongdoing, and a spokesman for Change to Win said the group had had no involvement or discussion with Mr. Blagojevich. "The idea of a position at Change to Win was totally an invention of the governor," the spokesman said.

Ms. Jarrett could not be reached for comment Tuesday. Mr. Obama's advisers made the decision on Tuesday essentially to remain silent and ignored criticism for doing so from Republicans, a strategy reminiscent of how the Bush administration reacted to the last high-profile case of Mr. Fitzgerald, who was the special prosecutor in the C.I.A. leak case. Still, David Axelrod, a senior adviser to Mr. Obama, issued a statement late Tuesday saying he had misspoken in comments he made in November that now seemed to contradict Mr. Obama's assertions that he had no contact with Mr. Blagojevich in the conversations over a replacement. "I know he's talked to the governor," Mr. Axelrod said in an interview with "Fox News Sunday" on Nov. 23. "And there are a whole range of names, many of which have surfaced." On Tuesday, Mr. Axelrod said he had been wrong. "They did not then or at any time discuss the subject," according to his statement.

The arrest leaves the fate of Mr. Obama's vacant Senate seat in limbo. Mr. Blagojevich, who may remain in office while charged, still has the power to name a successor to Mr. Obama, though Illinois political experts suggested that the Legislature might move quickly to impeach him — and questioned whether anyone would want an appointment so tainted.

Senator Richard J. Durbin, Democrat of Illinois, said, "No appointment by this governor under these circumstances could produce a credible replacement."

Mr. Jones said he would call the State Senate back into session to write a law to schedule a special election for the seat. And Illinois Republicans called for Mr. Blagojevich to resign immediately "for the good of the state," a possibility that would put Lt. Gov. Pat Quinn, a Democrat who has clashed with Mr. Blagojevich for years and who said Tuesday that they had last spoken in the summer of 2007, in charge.

Of the accusations against Mr. Blagojevich, Mr. Quinn said he was astonished, adding, "Pray for every person and every family in Illinois."

Mr. Blagojevich arrived in office in 2002, portraying himself as a fresh break from the investigations that had plagued the state for years — and most recently from the investigation and eventual conviction of Gov. George Ryan, a Republican whom Mr. Blagojevich succeeded.

Last month, Mr. Blagojevich said that despite his regular criticism of Mr. Ryan over the years, he believed that President Bush should commute Mr. Ryan's 6 ½-year sentence even though he had served less than 13 months. It would be a "fine decision," Mr. Blagojevich said.

On Monday, Mr. Blagojevich, who was visiting a factory sit-in here in Chicago, said he was unconcerned about reports of the corruption investigations that have swirled around his administration since at least 2005 and have swept up 14 other people.

"I don't believe there's any cloud that hangs over me," he told reporters at the factory. "I think there's nothing but sunshine hanging over me."

Mr. Blagojevich seemed not to mind earlier news reports that his conversations had been recorded. "I should say if anybody wants to tape my conversations, go right ahead, feel free to do it," he said, though he added that those who carried out such recordings sneakily, "I would remind them that it kind of smells like Nixon and Watergate."

2

CAUSES OF CORRUPTION

Two powerful forces keep stoking the fires of corruption:
selfishness **and **greed*.

What Are the Causes of Corruption? Why do people choose to be corrupt rather than honest?
For some, being corrupt may be the easiest way-or indeed the only way-to get what they want.

Corruption in politics is an age-old problem for which no lasting solution has been found – despite many attempts. The democratic system of government was created to give power to the people and to root out corruption through legal checks and balances on government power. The practice in democracies of replacing officials every four to five years was designed to contain and control corruption and abuse of position.

At times, a bribe may provide a convenient means of avoiding punishment. Many who observe that politicians, policemen, and judges seem to ignore corruption or even practice it themselves merely follow their example.

For some, being corrupt may be the easiest way-or indeed the only way-to get what they want. At times, a bribe may provide a convenient means of avoiding punishment. Many who observe that politicians, policemen, and judges seem to ignore corruption or even practice it themselves merely follow their example.

As corruption snowballs, it becomes more acceptable until it is finally a way of life.

People with pitifully low wages come to feel that they have no option. They have to demand bribes if they want to make a decent living. And when those who extort bribes or pay them to gain an unfair advantage go unpunished, few are prepared to swim against the tide. "Because sentence against a bad work has not been executed speedily, that is why the heart of the sons of men has become fully set in them to do badly," observed King Solomon.-Ecclesiastes 8:11.

Two powerful forces keep stoking the fires of corruption: **selfishness **and **greed***.

Because of selfishness, corrupt people turn a blind eye to the suffering that their corruption inflicts on others, and they justify bribery simply because they benefit from it. The more material benefits they amass, the greedier those practices of corruption become. "A mere lover of silver will not be satisfied with silver," observed Solomon, "neither any lover of wealth with income." (Ecclesiastes 5:10)

Granted, greed may be good for making money, but it invariably winks at corruption and illegality.

Causes of Corruption

First, the motivation to earn higher income is extremely strong, compounded by poverty and by low and declining civil service salaries. Second, opportunities to engage in corruption are numerous. Given the government intervention in several aspects of economic life, rent-seeking and the discretion of many public officials is broad in developing countries. Third, accountability is typically weak, political competition and civil liberties are restricted, laws and penalties are poorly developed and enforced.

Low wages of government employees is often cited as a major inducement for corrupt behavior in the government. First, when low paid employees meet wealthier private sector clients, the wide difference in living standards between the two groups provides an inducement for corruption so as to climb the social ladder (catch up with Jones'). Second, high wages if paid to the government employees effectively work as fines for bribe-taking and act as 'efficiency wage' that could deter corrupt behavior. However, in a country, where corruption is harder to eliminate, there may be higher public sector wages and more bureaucracy (and high corruption) all at the same time. Another cause not related to wages, is whether governments intervene to redress market failures or for furthering their own careers and wealth.

The causes can be quite complex, including rational but inconsistent human behavior (as proclaimed by behavioral economists). For example, if by paying a bribe, I can avoid non-compliance with pollution regulations or tax payments, I will be tempted to try this approach. Similarly, if I am an honest firm and the inspector is trying to extort a bribe, I will be equally tempted to evade paying taxes. Also, there may be several layers in government and collusion between supervisor and inspector combined with an inept judiciary will leave the citizen with little choice but to pay bribes.
What is the optimal wage and commission rate to prevent bribery and ensure higher monitoring and truthfully reporting (say of pollution levels or tax evasion)? When greed exceeds penalty for taking bribes or compensation for truthful reporting, what is the outcome? Only large penalty for bribery tends to contain corruption because providing commission or incentives can induce truthful reporting or can lead to over-reporting by the corruption inspection about the firms' pollution level (leading to extortion). Rockingham and Weder (1997) find that in a study of 28 countries when wages were higher then in the manufacturing sector, there was a lower level of corruption. Other studies did not find a strong support for this negative relationship between relative wages and corruption.

There is some evidence that countries dependent upon extraction of natural resources have higher economic rents which is a breeding ground for higher corruption. Similarly, highly-aided countries (higher per capita aid flows) generate rents and lead to corruption. While one study has found that higher educational spending does not coincide with higher corruption, other studies indicate that social sectors and infrastructure sector (compared with agriculture, industry, and services sectors) are prone to higher corruption because these are largely financed by aid and involve 'brick and mortar' activities.

Corruption varies across countries as well as within countries. In a study of 8 countries to explain the pattern of corruption across public agencies using micro-data, Recantini et al (2005) found that (i) the internal design of the organization is systematically associated with perceptions of corruption, both by agency insiders and by its customers; (ii) corruption is lower when internal decisions on budget, procurement and personnel are regularly audited, and when these same decisions are taken with open and transparent procedures. Corruption in personnel is also lower when such decisions are based on merit and clearly stated professional criteria.

Corruption in local government

The term local government can mean different things depending on what system of government is being used. The basic concept is a district that has the authority and power of local self-government. Usually, local governments must answer to or share authority with the national government, central government, or federal government, but again this depends on what type of government exists in that area. A self governing district is called a municipality in political terms. Municipalities can consist of one or more regions, states, provinces, cities, towns, villages, or counties.

Local public officials who hold positions of power in a municipality many times misuse or abuse their power for dishonest or unlawful gain. The improper use of influence, power, or other means for private gain is called corruption. Citizens and voters may have a slightly different view of political corruption and may think of it as when a candidate promises something they are not planning on following through with. Opportunities to engage in corruption are numerous in local governments because of the many personal relationships involved and the trust given to local governing officials.

Certain demographic factors may exist within a municipality that can lead to or encourage corruption within a local government. Demographic factors pertain to demography which is the study of human population statistics, changes, and trends including personal characteristics of humans like population size, migration, age, gender, social class, level of education, race, religion, occupation, and family status. Because there are many factors that can lead to corruption in local government it is hard to study corruption patterns empirically, but recently, improved research strategies and information sources have made such studies better.

Since the ultimate source of rent - seeking behavior is the *availability* of rents, corruption is likely to occur where restrictions and government intervention lead to the presence of such excessive profit

Examples include trade restrictions (such as tariff s and import quotas), favoritism industrial policies (such as subsidies and tax deductions), price controls, multiple exchange rate practices and foreign exchange allocation schemes, and government – controlled provision of credit. Some rents may arise in the Absence of government intervention, as in the case of natural re sources, such as oil, whose supply is limited by nature and whose extraction cost is far lower than its market price. Since abnormal profits are available to those who extract oil, officials who allocate extraction rights are likely to be offered bribes? Finally, one would expect that corruption is more likely to take place when civil servants are paid very low wages and often must resort to collecting bribes in order to feed their families.

While all of the hypotheses described above are empirically testable, in the sense that data are available for that purpose, only a few have actually been tested. What empirical studies have been done support certain hypotheses:

26

namely, that there is less corruption where there are fewer trade restrictions; where governments do not engage in favoritism industrial policies; and perhaps where natural resources are more abundant; and that there is somewhat less corruption where civil servants are paid better, compared with similarly qualified workers in the private sector (Van Rijckeghem and Weder, 1997).

Types of Corruption Found in Local Government

There are several types of political corruption that occur in local government. Some are more common than others, and some are more prevalent to local governments than to larger segments of government. Local governments may be more susceptible to corruption because interactions between private individuals and officials happen at greater levels of intimacy and with more frequency at more decentralized levels. Forms of corruption pertaining to money like bribery, extortion, embezzlement, and graft are found in local government systems. Other forms of political corruption are nepotism and patronage systems. One historical example was the Black Horse Cavalry a group of New York state legislators accused of blackmailing corporations.

Bribery is the offering of something which is most often money but can also be goods or services in order to gain an unfair advantage. Common advantages can be to sway a person's opinion, action, or decision, reduce amounts fees collected, speed up a government grants, or change outcomes of legal processes.

Extortion is threatening or inflicting harm to a person, their reputation, or their property in order to unjustly obtain money, actions, services, or other goods from that person. Blackmail is a form of extortion.

Embezzlement is the illegal taking or appropriation of money or property that has been entrusted to a person but is actually owned by another. In political terms this is called graft which is when a political office holder unlawfully uses public funds for personal purposes.

Nepotism is the practice or inclination to favor a group or person who is a relative when giving promotions, jobs, raises, and other benefits to employees. This is often based on the concept of families which is believing that a person must always respect and favor family in all situations including those pertaining to politics and business. This leads some political officials to give privileges and positions of authority to relatives based on relationships and regardless of their actual abilities.

Patronage systems consist of the granting favors, contracts, or appointments to positions by a local public office holder or candidate for a political office in return for political support. Many times patronage is used to gain support and votes in elections or in passing legislation. Patronage systems disregard the formal rules of a local government and use personal instead of formalized channels to gain an advantage.

A visibly disgusted FBI special agent Robert Grant stood at a podium in Chicago during a press conference Tuesday announcing the arrest of Gov. Rod Blagojevich and hurling his contempt at the entire political culture of the state of Illinois. "If it is not the most corrupt state in the United States, it's certainly one hell of a competitor," Grant said, his disheveled shock of black hair giving some indication of the dramatic and stressful events of the day. U.S. Attorney Patrick Fitzgerald termed the events leading up to the governor's early-morning arrest by the FBI, "a corruption crime spree," and said it was "an appalling statement about what's been happening in Illinois government."

So just what is the problem with Illinois?

It certainly seems like Illinois has a particular sweet spot for corruption: Blagojevich's own predecessor as governor, George Ryan, went to jail in 2007 in a 6-1/2 year sentence for corruption of his own. And two other Illinois governors have faced legal trouble in modern times: Otto Kerner, who was mocked locally as "Blotto Otto," and Dan Walker, who was charged in a savings and loan scheme involving fraudulent loans for repairs on his yacht, which was called The Governor's Lady. Fitzgerald, who is known as a crusading prosecutor for his role in the Valerie Plame CIA leak case, seemed to throw up his hands in despair, says: "We're not going to end corruption in Illinois by arrests and indictments alone." He stressed that rooting out corruption would depend on the willingness of the people of Illinois to solve the problem. In that, Fitzgerald may be on to something. It turns out that a state's culture is at least as important to its degree of corruption as the aggressiveness of its law enforcement officers. And it's also true that some states are just plain more corrupt than others. In an early attempt to explain why that is, the late Temple University political science professor Daniel J. Elazar argued in the 1960s that the United States can be divided in to three general political cultures, moralistic, traditional and individualistic. In a moralistic culture, the professor argued, government is considered to be a good thing, and officeholders expected to look out for the general welfare. In a traditional culture, citizens expect a hierarchical society. And individualistic cultures value private efforts over collective ones. Broadly defined, the moralistic areas of the US were New England and the Midwest, the Traditional areas were clustered in the south, and individualistic culture centered on the Atlantic seaboard in states like New York, New Jersey, Pennsylvania, Ohio and … Illinois.

It's the individualistic states, where there is an ethos that encourages people to be out for they, where corruption most easily takes root, argue some political scientists. Just look at the states that make up the group: "That's the corruption rogues gallery," says Colgate University political science professor Michael Johnston. "Every state has its own flavor," he says, "but they all have a very high level of risk for corruption." But the regional theory has one big flaw: The most corrupt states aren't in the "individualistic" part of the country. In 2007, the publication Corporate Crime Reporter crunched Department of Justice statistics to rank the 35 most populous states of the nation by corruption. The top three? Louisiana, Mississippi and Kentucky – which can be better thought of as broadly representing the "moralistic" states. Illinois didn't even break the top five, coming in sixth on the list. What gives? Colgate's Johnston says that there's more to it than just regional character. He's been studying political corruption since the 1970s, and has concluded that there are several key ingredients for political corruption. He says those include multiple political cultures competing for dominance, such as rural versus urban voters, tightly balanced party competition, and an elite political culture in which politicians expect to see corruption in their daily lives. "Corruption becomes a self fulfilling prophecy," Johnston says. "There's a real qualitative change when people walk out the door of their home each morning expecting to have to make payoffs." That certainly seems to be the case in Illinois. The scandal involving Otto Kerner Jr., for example, only came to light because one of the participants deducted the value of bribes paid in the 1960s--to win freeway exits and other favorable treatment for her horse track—in her income tax returns. The logic was that the payments were simply a part of doing business in Illinois. By the time the payments for services rendered came to light in the 1970s, Kerner was a federal judge and resigned in the scandal. With that kind of political tradition, Blagojevich may have presumed that he'd find a receptive audience for his alleged pay-to-play entreaties to other Illinois political figures. And just a few days ago, The Chicago Tribune reported that Fitzgerald had been shocked that a federal sting uncovered a ring of Illinois police officers who had allegedly participated in what they thought was a drug ring – even going so far as to help offload and deliver packages they believed to contain drugs from airplanes landing at an airport in the states. "When drug dealers deal drugs, they ought to be afraid of the police – not turn to them for help," Fitzgerald said at the time.

Not only does corruption seem to be concentrated in certain states, it also seems to go in waves throughout history. Louisiana, the most corrupt state in the nation, has a long and colorful history with political vice. "I steal money," legendary Democratic Gov. Huey Long once boasted to an audience at Louisiana State University in the 1930s, "but a lot of what I stole has spilled over in no-toll bridges, hospitals and to build this university."Long was assassinated in 1935. His successor as governor, Richard Leche, was forced to resign amidst a string of high level scandals but was sent to prison afterwards for his part in a scheme to sell trucks to the Louisiana Highway Department. Louisiana Gov. Edwin Edwards was pursued by prosecutors for virtually his entire four terms. He relished the image of a populist rogue, and contended that voters in Louisiana didn't care about conventional corruption. The only way to lose an election, he famously cracked, was to be "found in bed with a dead girl or a live boy." In 1988 he was convicted and sent to Federal prison after being found guilty of racketeering, extortion and money laundering in connection with help he provided Edward J. DeBartolo, Jr., in securing a casino license. Maryland, part of that Atlantic coast "individualistic" culture, had an amazing run of corruption of its own in the 1960's and 70s. During that period some 15 high elected officials were convicted of political corruption, the most famous being Spiro T. Agnew, who resigned as Richard Nixon's vice-president in 1972 after pleading no contest to charges of accepting tens of thousands of dollars in cash from contractors in exchange for state contracts. Agnew's successor, Marvin Mandel, took office as Governor in January, 1974 promising that the state would no longer be "a

postmark for greed, for corruption, for kickbacks and payoffs."
Three years later he was convicted on Federal charges of
accepting roughly $350,000 in gifts and favors from close
friends in exchange for state contracts and sent to prison.
Mandel's conviction was overturned after he served his
sentence when the Supreme Court said the law under which
he was prosecuted was being misused. It became clear during
that investigation that bribery had become part of the business
model for many state and county contractors, and in quick
succession, the county executives of suburban Baltimore
County and Anne Arundel County were indicted and convicted
of similar crimes. One of the more candid of those officials,
then-Anne Arundel County Executive Joseph Alton, said in
interviews at the time that he had simply been playing by the
rules as understood in Maryland at the time. "It's like I got
caught going 35 in a 30 mile zone," he said. New Jersey,
another so-called "individualistic" state, also has an infamous
political culture. U.S. Attorney Christopher Christie, based in
Newark, prosecuted more than 130 public officials during his
seven years in office. Among them were the mayors or
executives of Paterson, Irvington, and North Bergen, Essex
County and Newark itself as well as the president of the State
Senate. Just last month, another powerful former New Jersey
State Senator was convicted of procuring millions of state
dollars for a state university in exchange for a phony job there
that helped him triple his state pension. "Like Turnpike traffic
and the stink from the Linden oil fields, political corruption is
one of those ugly aspects of life in New Jersey," the Newark
Star-Ledger said recently, as it produced a multi-media
"rogues gallery' of recently-convicted office-holders.
Colgate University's Johnston says one good thing about
making a career of studying political corruption is that it never
goes away. "You never run out of things to talk about," he
said. "And everywhere I've been in the United States, people
say, 'If you want to learn about political corruption, come to
our town."

Crony Capitalism

Crony capitalism is a pejorative term describing an allegedly capitalist economy in which success in business depends on close relationships between businesspeople and government officials. It may be exhibited by favoritism in the distribution of legal permits, government grants, special tax breaks, and so forth.

Crony capitalism is believed to arise when political cronyism spills over into the business world; self-serving friendships and family ties between businessmen and the government influence the economy and society to the extent that it corrupts public-serving economic and political ideals.

Crony Capitalism in Practice

In its lightest form, crony capitalism consists of collusion among market players. While perhaps lightly competing against each other, they will present a unified front to the government in requesting subsidies or aid (sometimes called a trade association or industry trade group). Newcomers to a market may find it difficult to find loans or acquire shelf space to sell their product; in technological fields, they may be accused of infringing on patents that the established competitors never invoke against each other. Distribution networks will refuse to aid the entrant. That said, there will still be competitors who "crack" the system when the legal barriers are light, especially where the old guard has become inefficient and is failing to meet the needs of the market. Of course, some of these upstarts may then join with the established networks to help deter any other new competitors. Examples of this have been argued to include the *keiretsu* of post-war Japan, the *chaebol* of South Korea, and the powerful families who control much of the investment in Latin America.

Crony capitalism is generally associated with more virulent government intervention, however. Intentionally ambiguous laws and regulations are common in such systems. Taken strictly, such laws would greatly impede practically all business; in practice, they are only erratically enforced. The specter of having such laws suddenly brought down upon a business provides incentive to stay in the good graces of political officials. Troublesome rivals who have overstepped their bounds can have the laws suddenly enforced against them, leading to fines or even jail time. States often said to exhibit crony capitalism include the People's Republic of China; India, especially up to the early 1990s when the manufacturing was strictly controlled by the Central Government, giving rise to the phrase of "License Raj"; Indonesia; Mexico; Brazil; Malaysia; Russia; and most other ex-Soviet states. Critics claim that government connections are almost indispensable to business success in these countries. Wu Jinglian, one of China's leading economists and a longtime champion of its transition to free markets, says that it faces two starkly contrasting futures: a market economy under the rule of law or crony capitalism.

Cronyism in sections of an economy

More direct government involvement can lead to specific areas of crony capitalism, even if the economy as a whole may be healthy. Governments will, often in good faith, establish government agencies to regulate an industry. However, the members of an industry have a very strong interest in the actions of a regulatory body, while the rest of the citizenry are only lightly affected. As a result, it is not uncommon for current industry players to gain control of the "watchdog" and use it against competitors. This phenomenon is known as regulatory capture. A famous early example in the United States would be the Interstate Commerce Commission, which was established in 1887 to regulate the railroad "robber barons;" instead, it quickly became controlled by the railroads, which set up a permit system that was used to deny access to new entrants and functionally legalized price fixing.[4] A more modern example would be the case of Creekstone Farms. After the mad cow scare, Creekstone decided to test all its cows for mad cow disease. This would enable them to sell again to Japan, which had blocked import of all American beef that had not been completely tested. After the proper facilities had been built and the personnel hired to make such a change, the U.S. Department of Agriculture issued an injunction and refused to allow Creekstone to buy the kits necessary to test.[5] This allowed the larger beef producers to keep costs low and not be out-competed by a smaller rival. Creekstone sued the USDA in response for abrogating free competition in the market. Economist Paul Krugman commented that the incident showed that "the imperatives of crony capitalism trump[ed] professed faith in free markets," at least for the Department of Agriculture at the time.

The military-industrial complex in the United States is often described as an example of crony capitalism in an industry. Connections with The Pentagon and lobbyists in Washington are described by critics as more important than actual competition, due to the political and secretive nature of defense contracts. In the Airbus-Boeing WTO dispute, Airbus (which receives subsidies from European governments outright) has stated Boeing receives similar subsidies, which are hidden as inefficient defense contracts. In another example, Bechtel, claiming that it should have had a chance to bid for certain contracts, said Halliburton had received no-bid contracts due to having cronies in the Bush administration. Gerald P. O'Driscoll former vice president at the Federal Reserve Bank of Dallas stated that Fannie Mae and Freddie Mac became classic examples of crony capitalism. Government backing let Fannie and Freddie dominate mortgage underwriting. "The politicians created the mortgage giants, which then returned some of the profits to the pols -

sometimes directly, as campaign funds; sometimes as "contributions" to favored constituents."

Creation of Crony Capitalism in Developing Economies

In its worst form, crony capitalism can devolve into simple corruption, where any pretense of a free market is dispensed with. Bribes to government officials are considered *de rigueur* and tax evasion is common; this is seen in many parts of Africa, for instance. This is sometimes called plutocracy (rule by wealth) or kleptocracy (rule by theft). Corrupt governments may favor one set of business owners who have close ties to the government over others. This may also be done with racial, religious, or ethnic favoritism; for instance, Alawites in Syria have a disproportionate share of power in the government and business there. (President Assad is an Alawite.) This can be explained by considering personal relationships as a social network. As government and business leaders try to accomplish various things, they naturally turn to other powerful people for support in their endeavors. These people form hubs in the network. In a developing country those hubs may be very few, thus concentrating economic and political power in a small interlocking group.

Normally, this will be untenable to maintain in business; new entrants will affect the market. However, if business and government are entwined, then the government can maintain the small-hub network.

Political Viewpoints

Critics of capitalism including Socialists and other anti-capitalists often assert that crony capitalism is the inevitable result of *any* capitalist system. Jane Jacobs described it as a natural consequence of collusion between those managing power and trade. Since businesses make money and money leads to political power, business will inevitably use their power to influence governments. Much of the impetus behind campaign finance reform in the United States and in other countries is an attempt to prevent economic power being used to take political power.

Capitalists oppose crony capitalism as well, but consider it an aberration brought on by governmental favors incompatible with true capitalism. In this view, crony capitalism is the result of an excess of socialist-style interference in the market, which requires active corporate lobbying to reduce red tape. These advocates point to the relatively higher levels of interaction between corporations and governments that are considered more socialist, taken to its maximum in the form of nationalization of industries. Even if the initial regulation was well-intentioned (to curb actual abuses), and even if the initial lobbying by corporations was well-intentioned (to reduce illogical regulations), the mixture of business and government eventually proves poisonous. In his book *The Myth of the Robber Barons*, Burton W. Folsom, Jr. distinguished those that engage in crony capitalism – designated by him "political entrepreneurs" – from those who compete in the marketplace without special aid from government, whom he calls "market entrepreneurs." Economists of the Austrian School also oppose crony capitalism, calling it "state corporatism" to emphasize the role of the state in the problem as well. Socialist economists have criticized the term as an ideologically motivated attempt to cast what are in their view the fundamental problems of capitalism as avoidable irregularities. The term "crony capitalism" made its first significant impact in the public arena as an explanation of the Asian financial crisis. This explanation is frequently dismissed as apologetics for failures of neoliberal policy and more fundamental weaknesses of market allocation. According to socialist economist Robin Hahnel, IMF officials Michel Camdessus and Stanley Fischer were quick to explain that the afflicted economies had only themselves to blame. Crony capitalism, lack of transparency, accounting procedures not up to international standards, and weak-kneed politicians too quick to spend and too afraid to tax were the problems according to IMF and US Treasury Department officials. The fact that the afflicted economies had been held up as paragons of virtue and IMF/World Bank success stories only a year before, the fact that neoliberals' only success story had been the Newly Industrialized Countries (NIC's) who were now in the tank, and the fact that the IMF and Treasury department story just didn't fit the facts since the afflicted economies were no more rife with crony capitalism, lack of transparency, and weak-willed politicians than dozens of other economies untouched by the Asian financial crisis, simply did not matter.

Finally, some critics question whether the concept is meaningful at all, pointing out that personal factors influence business decisions in all economic systems that involve a government and that the existence of these factors is an insufficient explanation for why certain economic systems work better than others.

Campaign contributions

In the political arena, it is difficult to prove corruption. For this reason, there are often unproved rumors about many politicians, sometimes part of a smear campaign.
Politicians are placed in apparently compromising positions because of their need to solicit financial contributions for their campaign finance. If they then appear to be acting in the interests of those parties that funded them, this gives rise to talk of political corruption. Supporters may argue that this is coincidental. Cynics wonder why these organizations fund politicians at all, if they get nothing for their money.

Laws regulating campaign finance in the United States require that all contributions and their use should be publicly disclosed. Many companies, especially larger ones, fund both the Democratic and Republican parties. Certain countries, such as France, ban altogether the corporate funding of political parties. Because of the possible circumvention of this ban with respect to the funding of political campaigns, France also imposes maximum spending caps on campaigning; candidates that have exceeded those limits, or that have handed misleading accounting reports, risk having their candidacy ruled invalid, or even be prevented from running in future elections. In addition, the government funds political parties according to their successes in elections. In some countries, political parties are run solely off subscriptions (membership fees).

Even legal measures such as these have been argued to be legalized corruption, in that they often favor the political status quo. Minor parties and independents often argue that efforts to rein in the influence of contributions do little more than protect the major parties with guaranteed public funding while constraining the possibility of private funding by outsiders. In these instances, officials are legally taking money from the public coffers for their election campaigns to guarantee that they will continue to hold their influential and often well-paid positions.

Demographic factors Causing Corruption

Socioeconomic characteristics and the size of the population of people that make up a municipality can be encouraging factors for local government officials to engage in corrupt practices. Patterns of political corruption can be found in places that have a similar demographic make-up. Demographic factors that have been known to lead to or increase the likelihood of corruption in a local government system are religion, race, class, size of the municipality, local economic conditions, education, political culture, and gender. Some factors are interrelated or can lead to other factors which may cause more corruption.

Religion

Religions can influence how citizens place their loyalties, for instance, whether religion, family, community, or local government requires more involvement or is more important to them. The less involved citizens are in local politics, the less aware they are of corruption in local government, and thus the more corrupt a local system can be.

Race & Class

Social & urban segregation and abuse of political power in a municipality can lead to a more corrupt local government. The different areas of the municipality will have very different wants, needs, and ideas and therefore, will constantly struggle against each other for better representation in the local government and more favorable legislation for their area. Socially, racially, or ethnically divided municipalities tend to have more corrupt local officials and less organized systems. Governments with racial divisions will have internal antagonism and opposition between the different races and more incentive to use illegal means to gain advantages over the opposing side. Less organized government processes allow for more opportunities for corrupt practices to go unnoticed.

Size of a Municipality

Larger municipalities tend to encourage corruption to take place within a local government. Bigger municipalities require more local officials to represent and run the local government. With more officials, it is harder to keep tabs on each one and establish a decent administration and to monitor their activities. Large municipalities may also have inadequate or insufficient policing and prosecution of corrupt local officials. This also encourages corruption to occur in local government because there is less likelihood of either getting caught or prosecuted, therefore, more officials may become dishonest or at least be tempted to.

Condition of the Local Economy

Low economic development has been found to be an encouraging factor for political corruption. Economic practices like dependence on raw material industries and drug trades are characteristic of poorer cities and areas with increased amounts of corruption. Economic dependence on certain industries will also lead to less stable governments and less amount of money available to fund governments. Fragile economies lead to increased levels of poverty and less opportunities to get out of poverty. Poverty is a known factor that encourages corruption in local governments. Places with failing economies and poverty sometimes get loans or start aid programs to support the local economy and the people, and public officials are often able to unlawfully take the money or goods for private gain. With less money available, local officials are more likely to get lower wages which is seen as another factor that leads to corruption. Officials who get lower wages which are not enough to provide for their necessities, they will many times become corrupt and try something like embezzling money that may entrusted to them in the local treasury. Low wages can cause economic insecurity and encourage politicians to take advantage of current opportunities as a public figure of authority. On the other hand, some researchers argue that the more money a local government has to spend, the more tendency it will have to do so inefficiently, which can lead to suspicions of corruption. Overall, poorer municipalities are more often perceived to have corrupt local governments than rich ones.

Education

Lower levels of education which are often caused by poverty are seen as a factor which encourages corrupt government practices. With less amounts of education people are not informed as to how the government works or what rights they have under the government. It is easier for corrupt office-holders to conceal corrupt activities from a poorly educated public. Uneducated citizens are less likely to be aware of corruption in local governments or how to stop it, and therefore, corruption is able to remain and spread. Without some kind of political awareness, citizens will not know which candidates to elect that are honest or dishonest or other ways to prevent corruption from taking place in their local governments. This often leads municipalities to be continually governed by one or more corrupt local officials who use patronage or nepotistic practices to stay in office or keep influence in the government for long periods of time. When local political leaders are less educated, they will be less likely to find legitimate ways to make the municipality well-structured, productive, and successful.

Political Culture of the Municipality

Many local governments have an established political culture with certain expectations and practices that often determine what is seen as acceptable and not acceptable in local politics. In municipalities with an undeveloped or underdeveloped political culture, accountability and legitimacy is usually low and principles of ethics in government are not established. This can encourage corruption to take hold in the local government because citizens do not know what is considered corrupt, and local officials are not afraid to be corrupt because of the low accountability. In some places the local governments have been corrupt for so long that the citizens think that is how it is supposed to work because that is all they have been exposed to. Long periods of political instability will also lead to corruption in the government because people are unsure of how the government should operate, and thus do not know what practices are corrupt or how to stop them if they are corrupt.

Gender

Research shows that women are more trustworthy than men and are less likely to be corrupt. Women are less likely to agree with corrupt practices like bribery or take bribes. Having no or fewer women in the local government is another factor that may encourage corruption. Places that do not have policies to narrow gender gaps and give women equal rights in the government more commonly have less integrity and more corruption in them.

Ways to Stop and Prevent Corruption in Local Governments

- The most important thing is to resolve the underlying factors that cause corruption in local government.
- Continue to change the primary focus of global Anti-Corruption campaigns to local governments
- Because they are closest to citizens, transparency and accountability are the most important to the legitimacy of local officials
- It is simpler to find partners to stop corruption locally
- National politicians many times start off their political careers in the local government.
- Develop incentives that encourage honest governments by perhaps redesigning the terms of public employment
- Accountability-enhancing reforms and Civil service reform

- Strengthening the oversight and sanctions of local officials to improve accountability
- Anti-corruption monitoring groups or commissions
- Enforce existing anti-bribery legislation
- Create more policies to close the gender gap in public office holding

3
THE COST OF CORRUPTION

Cost of corruption by state officials high for Illinois taxpayers

The corruption in Illinois is so excessive, our state has become a national punch line. Blagojevich's national humiliation tour was the most recent event, but Illinois and Chicago have a long history of tolerating corruption.

In Chicago the phrase "vote early, vote often" is usually said with a laugh. It is also widely accepted the dead in Chicago rise every two or four years to vote. With the conviction of patronage chiefs Robert Sorich and the HDO's Al Sanchez, does any reasonable person think Mayor Daley is not complicit? These convictions occurred after the Shakman decree was signed stating the city would not partake in hiring based on political clout.

Even employees at the Board of Review which evaluates property tax assessments state it is a cesspool of corruption. It is stunning how this level of corruption is tolerated. Republicans are even culpable because they are terrified Jesse Jackson Jr. will become Mayor and immediately devolve into a race-baiting poverty pimp like his father. Some think the corruption is tolerated because it has slowly built up over time like a frog in a pot of water on a stove. Does this excuse the apathy?

At political events it is painful to hear the aphorism "people get the government they deserve." There is truth in this saying. There are always two ways at looking at voter disinterest. Either people are very happy with their lives or they are too self-absorbed to care about voting. Half of the people eligible to register to vote are registered. And half of the registered voters vote. Therefore, our elected officials win with 12.5% of the population supporting them.

One of the barriers to voting are people do not understand the true cost of corruption. Most Chicago residents think corruption is awarding snow removal contracts to the Mayor's friends. The awarding of clout contracts and no bid contracts is the 300% to 1000% increase in contract value to fair market. $300,000 value contracts are charged well in excess of $1million. Repeat this process thousands of times and you will start to see a massive budget gap developing. It is less of a concern that a politically connected person gets a city job (assuming they do it adequately) than the long-term impact of corrupt no bid contracts and their corresponding debt.

Governments operate at significantly less efficient levels than the free markets, but Chicago and Illinois governance essentially does not work. The state of Illinois is a year behind in paying their bills. Many Illinois businesses, especially pharmacies, will not take a check from the state of Illinois.

When patronage and no bid contracts go to a small circle of corrupt power hungry cronies, the needs of the people are not met. There would be revenue to renegotiate the police contracts if but for the corruption tax.

Public safety, mass transit infrastructure, education, and healthcare have all degraded to unacceptable levels because of the cost of corruption. Blagojevich is not the problem, merely a symptom. If voters do not hold elected officials to higher standards, expect more of the same.

Chicago is more dangerous than Baghdad. How many lives are lost every year as a cost of corruption? Less than 50% of Chicago Public School high school students graduate and less than 6% graduate from college. Patients go to Stroger hospital with bags of food because they know they will be there 2-3 meals before seeing a doctor. Our jails are overflowing. Public transit is falling apart. And we cannot afford police services.

This is the cost of corruption.

As taxpayers look down the barrel of a major income tax increase, another tax already is draining their wallets. But this one isn't found anywhere in the tax code.
It's the "corruption tax" -- the extra money Illinois residents pay because of dishonest public officials.

People pay the tax when politicians give government jobs to unqualified cronies and contracts to expense-padding donors. They pay when public employees take bribes to overlook violations, when law enforcement spends millions prosecuting crooked politicians and when people are injured because of government misconduct. "It means hundreds of millions of dollars lost in waste," said Dick Simpson, a former Chicago alderman and head of political science at the University of Illinois in Chicago. Every state has its share of bad apples, but Illinois is notoriously corrupt. Residents and politicians sometimes seem to embrace the state's "anything goes" culture. All together, 1,000 public officials and businessmen have been convicted of public corruption in Illinois since 1970, Simpson found. That includes 19 Cook County judges, 30 Chicago aldermen, two members of Congress and two governors plus another imprisoned for crimes unrelated to state government.

Then there's Gov. Rod Blagojevich, who was arrested in December on charges of trying to squeeze money out of candidates seeking an open U.S. senate seat. His arrest seemed ramp up anger over public corruption. It's impossible to calculate the full cost of the corruption tax. Simpson has come up with a $300 million estimate, but that focuses on the Chicago area and doesn't directly apply to taxpayer's downstate. Still, experts point too many ways corrupt government is more expensive than honest government.

Shoddy work

Someone put in a government job because he knows the right people isn't likely to work hard for his paycheck. In extreme cases, he might not show up for work at all, instead becoming what's known as a ghost pay roller. One Cicero "health inspector" got $133,000 in salary and benefits for a job he never performed. He also got a one-year prison sentence.

Likewise, a company awarded a city contract through bribery isn't going to worry about performance; a lousy job won't jeopardize contract renewal.

Just look at Chicago's "Hired Truck" program, where the city outsourced hauling jobs to private firms. Many companies, some with Mob connections, paid bribes to get contracts then collected taxpayer money while doing little or no work. A federal investigation has resulted dozens of corruption convictions.

Unnecessary expenses

When corrupt officials want to create work for political allies, they sometimes fill jobs that don't need to be filled or produce unnecessary "consulting" contracts. Just after Blagojevich became governor, the state suddenly started paying a company more than $500,000 to wash buildings, bridges and even road salt storage domes. Yet the work could have been done by state employees. The firm's president turned out to be the brother-in-law of a high-ranking Transportation Department official, who eventually resigned after the contract was suspended.

Law Enforcement

It costs money to catch a crook. FBI agents and U.S. attorneys can spend years -- and multiple criminal trials -- working their way up the corruption ladder to someone like Gov. George Ryan. First come the foot soldiers, then middle management, then high-ranking advisers and finally the top guy. Investigations of Ryan, for instance, stretch back to 1993.

The federal probe kicked into high gear in 1998, and Ryan was convicted in 2006. He's now serving 6{ years in prison.

Officials could not estimate the total cost of Ryan's case, but its clear their time and money could have been spent going after the mob or drug dealers or crooked businessmen. "Every time we have a federal prosecution, that's a cost," said Cindi Canary, executive director of the Illinois Campaign for Political Reform.

Outright Theft

Corruption doesn't always involve shady contracts and political scheming. Some people just steal. The former manager of an East St. Louis federal housing agency was convicted in 2006 for embezzling nearly $158,000. She spent most of the money on gambling. And an employee in the state treasurer's office was convicted of stealing at least $263,000 from taxpayers by opening a bank account under a false name and depositing state money in it.

Lost Business

Businesses weigh many factors when deciding where to locate or expand operations, including tax breaks and regulatory policies. They also look at the political climate. Businesses concerned they won't get their fair share of government services without paying bribes, or who think backroom deals dictate government policy, may very well decide Illinois isn't for them. "Businesses fear getting dragged into something that will get bad press or get involved in a federal or state investigation. That's huge," said George Ranney, president and CEO of Chicago Metropolis 2020. "If there's a real cloud, it's probably as important as tax breaks."

More businesses mean more jobs, and more money flowing into the state treasury to help take some of the burden off struggling families.

Corruption also can be a factor for smaller Illinois companies or entrepreneurs who hope to get businesses off the ground but hesitate to seek government contracts because they haven't donated to the right politician or greased the right palm. Taxpayers, in turn, miss out on competition for state work and businesses that could create jobs and pay taxes are weakened. The belief that government doors are closed to most people, whether ambitious entrepreneurs or just average taxpayers, hurts everyone, says Sen. Dan Cronin, R-Elmhurst. "People become hardened, they withdraw from the system, they don't follow what's going on," Cronin said. "Then what happens? It only gets worse because nobody's watching."

Costs and Benefits of Corruption

There is no evidence that corruption has any positive benefits. The argument that 'speed money' or 'grease the wheels' or 'grist that helps grind' is ultimately beneficial by cutting down red-tape and bureaucratic inefficiency has no empirical basis. It only creates opportunities at every level of bureaucracy and even honest officials are tempted to increase red-tapism by spreading and slowing down the processing of requests as the honest officials do not want to be responsible for any decision that they might regret in the future. If corruption was beneficial to society, one would have legalized such corrupt practices! How does one explain the high level of corruption in a large number of countries despite repressive laws to control it? Everyone now accepts that some level of corruption is inevitable in every mix of market and government. Politicians and bureaucrats have vested interest in increasing and over-extending themselves into market place to maximize corruption. Therefore, a minimalist state would be helpful in curbing corruption and corrupt practices.

There appears, however, to be a trade-off between government corruption and market failures. Governments intervene with the best of intentions in the case of 'market failures' and use subsidies and transfers as mechanisms to divert resources from gainers of market failures to losers or vulnerable groups. This creates corruption opportunities but corruption undermines the very purpose of government intervention. Government intervention requires bureaucrats (agents) to collection information, make decisions and implement policies and programs. This situation gives rise for self-interest of bureaucrats to kick-in by virtue of their information gathering duties and makes it hard to monitor their action properly. In addition, if the government is keen to control corruption, it will hire officials to prevent corruption. As such, there is a misallocation of talented individuals away from productive activity towards corruption control. All this means that corruption in the form of rents for bureaucrats induces a misallocation of resources and rapidly expands the size of the bureaucracy. Corruption is difficult to eliminate completely, which means that we are living in a 'second best' world, in which some bureaucrats will always be taking bribes.

The Cost of Corruption: Why You Should Care?

There are costs to widespread political corruption that go beyond the value of what is stolen, that go beyond the money spent on criminal investigations and trials, and that go beyond the public funds spent to incarcerate the guilty:

The loss of legitimacy of the political process

Corruption destroys public support for the political system. And the appearance of corruption is just as corrosive. If everyone believes Illinois politics is corrupt, there is no reason to accept
the policies or programs of government as having authority or value. If everyone believes that all Illinois politicians are corrupt, or become corrupt soon after they take office, then

there is no reason to support their attempts to promote individual responsibility, to solve the state's social problems, and to provide care for those in need.

The loss of citizen participation

Participation in politics is part of a civic culture that develops and ennobles individuals and society, making people better and society better. When citizens share in the decision-making and have a vested interest in the outcomes, the foundations of the political system are strong. A corrupt political system does not encourage participation, nor does a system in which politics is reserved for the professional politician. If everyone is a crook, why vote? When there is a widespread perception that politics is corrupt and someone else's business, the pool of citizens that participates, makes decisions, and influences policy grows smaller. The state loses, and individual citizens lose, when a corrupt political system limits and discourages political participation.

A weakening talent pool for government

A corrupt political system does not encourage young people to engage in politics or make politics a career. The process is poisoned by the perception, let alone the reality, that patronage hires and political interference make it difficult for talented people without political connections to get state or local jobs or do a professional job of delivering services. The resulting talent pool of those who want to get involved with government as a career keeps shrinking.

The deterioration of the quality of public services

Do-nothing jobs, make-work contracts, and inflated no-bid contracts take resources away from doing the real job of state and local government. The diversion of public resources to political or private ends make meeting the state's basic obligations of education, health and welfare, and protection of the environment increasingly more difficult. So does the inability to attract qualified people to public service. At the same time our political culture discourages the kinds of policy innovations and risk taking that leads to improved ways of addressing the state's obligations.

The High Cost of Corruption

What is the impact of corruption on a nation's economy?

Like heat, humidity, and tax rates, corruption falls into the "everything is relative" category. We happen to live in Boston, home of the Big Dig, said to be the second-largest public works project in history. The Big Dig, launched in 1991 to bury many of the city's highways and create a wide swath of parkland, was supposed to be concluded in 2001 for $2.8 billion. It may be done by 2010, with a final price tag of $14.6 billion. Now, anyone who has ever put in a new kitchen knows that renovations always cost twice what you expect, but an $11 billion overrun certainly seems to suggest that, yes, there is corruption in America. But it's rare—comparatively. We recently returned from a trip to Latin America where we met with hundreds of business people in Brazil and Argentina. Their stories of ubiquitous corruption, much of it at the hands of the government, were chilling. Tax evasion is widespread; enforcement is spotty. In Argentina, several CEOs told us that if you attempt to conduct business without playing by the unwritten rules imposed by layer after layer of government bureaucrats, an army of tax auditors arrives at your door, paralyzing your company and often times staying until an employee or two goes to jail. We don't mean to single out Latin America. Even in Europe, business-as-usual can include illegal activities. Yes, the situation has improved in the past decade. But European CEOs have told us that bribery was once so pervasive—in Germany, bribes were legal through most of the '90s—that they often did not know which of their own employees they could trust. Today, corruption is particularly rampant in the developing world, from India to China, and through Eastern Europe to Russia. It remains one of the main reasons that capitalism cannot take root in Africa. Corruption can make it just too expensive to start a business, or in many cases, to keep a small one running. By contrast, the relative lack of corruption in the U.S. is a key reason, along with an entrepreneurial culture and the wide availability of venture capital, that we lead the world in business creation. Virtually no one starting a company in the U.S. today, and no one funding one, has to worry about covering the hidden costs of bribes, payoffs, and kickbacks. They just have to worry about coming up with great ideas, getting the best people, and delivering a terrific execution. That's hard enough!

Yes, the U.S. has its share of corruption in public works projects. And we did have a spate of corporate scandals—Enron, WorldCom, and Tyco, to name the most notorious. But those were mainly cases of individual fraud and malfeasance, not systemic corruption. We really don't have that. Which is why when you compare the sustained health and entrepreneurial energy of the American economy with the more corrupt countries around the world, your question says it all: Corruption is a competitive disadvantage.

If the costs of corruption are so high, why don't governments get rid of it?

A possible answer is that once a corrupt system is in place, and a majority of people operate within that system, individuals have no incentive to try to change it or tore f rain from taking part in it, even if everybody would be better off if corruption were to be eliminated. Consider the following examples:

• You live in a society where everybody steals. Do you choose to steal? The probability that you will be caught is low, because the police are very busy chasing other thieves, and, even if you do get caught, the chances of you are being punished severely for a crime that is so common is low. Therefore, you too steal. By contrast, if you u l live in a society where theft is rare, the chances of your being caught and punished are high, so you choose not to steal.

• You are a new junior civil servant in an administration where everybody, including your superiors, is very corrupt. Somebody offers you a bribe to help him avoid paying taxes. You decline the offer. A few hours later, you receive a telephone call from your boss, who would have liked a cut of your bribe. Your boss suggests that if you treat a friend nicely (by accepting the bribe), you may be promoted, while if you don't, you will be transferred to a remote provincial office. You then take the bribe and share it with your boss and colleagues. If, instead , the administration in which you work is very honest, you are likely to behave honestly to avoid the risk of being fired.

• Individuals A and B are members of the same government. Suppose, on the one hand, that A is very corrupt and has established a private bribe-collection system for her own gain. The need to pay substantial bribes reduces entrepreneurs' incentives to invest and imposes a significant burden on economic growth. Citizens realize that economic growth is being harmed by the corrupt government, though they may not know exactly who is soliciting bribes. Therefore, they decide not to reelect the government. This shortens B's horizon, making him more inclined to extract a large proportion of current output and to disregard any ensuing adverse effects on future output. In other words, B will seek to obtain a large slice of the cake today since he knows that the government that he participates in will soon be ousted. On the other hand, following similar line of reasoning, if *A* does not collect bribes, then *B* will also refrain from doing so.

The last example may provide an explanation not only for the persistence of corruption but also for the empirical observation those, on average, countries that are more corrupt tend to be more politically unstable. It also suggests that both corruption and political instability may result from the failure of members of the same government or ruling elite to coordinate their actions. In that sense, corruption and political instability may be two sides of the same coin. This example may fit the cases of countries that are bedeviled by frequent coups whereby corrupt regimes succeed one another. At the same time, it does not explain a number of other relevant cases, such as those of dictators who have remained in power for many years by allowing their supporters to collect large bribes, or those of governments formed by groups of individuals who have been able to agree on bribe levels that are high, but not so high as to cause them tube ousted.

All of the above examples show that once corruption has become ingrained, it is very difficult to get rid of. As a result, corruption tends to persist, together with its adverse consequences. This leads to an import antipolice conclusion, which is consistent with international experience over the past few decades. Attempts to eliminate corruption tend to succeed when reforms are undertaken in a very sudden and forceful manner and are supported at the highest levels of government. However, an equally relevant question is what characteristics make countries more likely to fall into a high-corrupt ption,low growth trap.

The Cost of corruption is Immeasurable

The money paid some top officials of the ministry of communications, including ministers over a four year period was put at over US $10 million dollars. This figure paid the Nigerians that were directly involved in contract processes that led to the award of several communications contract to Siemens during the period, is generally the cost attached to corruption. However, Business Day investigations last week can now reveal that for every corrupt activity, the actual cost is immeasurable. In the case of bribery, which is arguably the most popular type of corruption, the face value is the actual bribe paid to a government official. And this is usually described as the cost, but the entire cost can only be imagined if it is considered that the bribe will not be given if the benefit derived is equal to or less. So, for Siemens to give the bribe of over US $10 million, it is conceivable that the benefit to the company is much more. In actual sense, the total cost of the corrupt activity is the total benefit that would have accrued to the country, including the value of investment, jobs, and the economic growth lost.

Last year, the money stolen from Nigeria's treasury between 1960 and 1999 was estimated at more than US $440 billion, more than our present annual Gross Domestic Product (GDP). If the figure is a realistic estimate of the money stolen, as staggering as it seems, it is less than the actual cost to Nigeria. It does not include the returns on investment in education that would have been bought, the loss of lives that would have been prevented by improved healthcare, the cost of damaged vehicles and loss of lives due to bad roads, and many condemned future of individuals very difficult to identify. Why is the cost of corruption in Nigeria immeasurable? First, as widespread as it seems in Nigeria, corruption is actually a hidden and secretive engagement between two or more individuals, with one for the purpose of personal gain but dispensing a public benefit. So, except caught or some certain level of extrapolation is conducted, the activity may never be known. The immeasurability of corruption is complicated by the distinction between direct and indirect cost that are attributable to corruption. Bribes are direct cost but this aspect is very marginal. Indirect costs are huge because of the areas in which the corrupt activities are perpetrated. For instance, the indirect cost of Siemens contracts include the reduction in the quality and quantity of work that would have been done, the costs forgone in terms of benefits that the work would have brought about and the impact of the work on other businesses, investments, jobs and economic performance. What is the cost of our underdevelopment? To understand how corruption has contributed to underdevelopment and that our underdevelopment is the cost we pay for corruption over the years is to estimate the opportunity cost of all past corrupt activities in the country. The opportunity cost of corruption is what we would have if we did not have the corruption, and this is simply immense. Development would have benefited from resources diverted, withheld or deterred, all due to corrupt activities. It is not inconceivable that this may be up to a quarter of our GDP a year, especially since the 1980s that the level of corruption escalated. Though a simplistic correlation between underdevelopment and corruption in government and the oil sector, Nigeria has a lower income per person now than it did before oil was discovered.

William Hale Thompson, who served as Chicago's mayor from 1915-23 and again from 1927-31, was rumored to be on the payroll of gangster Al Capone.

Dan Walker was Illinois governor from 1973-77.
Walker's crimes were committed after he served as governor
from 1973 to 1977. The Democrat and World War II and
Korean War veteran was convicted of fraud related to his
stewardship of the First American Savings & Loan Association
of Oak Brook. News reports at the time indicated that he
received more than $1 million in fraudulent loans for his
business and repairs on his yacht, the "Governor's Lady."

Former Gov. Otto Kerner Jr. was sentenced to three years in prison for bribery and related charges.

Ryan's downfall spurred both the election of Blagojevich, who campaigned as a reformer, and another round of reform talk. All this was just another example of how reform gets turned on its head.

For many taxpayers, the charges against former Gov. Rod Blagojevich reinforce the belief that Illinois residents have been paying taxes to a corrupt government for years - spending their hard-earned money on patronage hires, wasteful contracts and inefficient bureaucracies.

4

PREVENTION OF CORRUPTION

Prevention: An Effective Tool to Reduce Corruption in the
Illinois Government &
Lessons From Around the World

The anti-corruption strategy advocated in this book rests on four pillars: (a) economic development; (b) democratic reform; (c) a strong civil society with access to information and a mandate to oversee the state; and (d) the presence of rule of law., The governance program facilitates, at the request of client Governments, a series of anti-corruption anti/integrity workshops, seminars, and surveys involving broad segments of society, and national and local Government. Such instruments have served to empower civil society and improve service delivery through greater transparency and accountability. Working in partnership with governments and civil society, the program continues to help develop National Integrity Systems in Africa, Europe and Central Asia, and the Middle East and North Africa. These systems facilitate the building of awareness, prevention of corrupt practices, prosecution of corrupt officials, and reward of honest civil servants at all levels of government.

On the basis of these four broad contexts, there are four basic arenas in which action can be taken against corruption within a country:

First, the basic institution of good governance needs to be strengthened. At the head of this list is the judiciary, which is itself the guardian of laws and integrity. But if the judiciary is itself corrupt, the problem is compounded and the public at large without rule of law.

Second, the capacity and integrity of enforcement need to be enhanced. The best law has no value if it is not enforced. The best judges and magistrates are wasted if cases are never brought to them. Good investigations are wasted effort if the judge or magistrate is corrupt.

Third, a government needs to put in place a solid set of preventive tools. Codes of Conduct and strong independent oversight bodies can help ensure that the acceptable standards of behavior are respected in both the private and public sector. Political leaders in all branches of government, legislative and judiciary can be required to have transparency in their own financial dealings through asset disclosure for themselves and their family members.

Fourth, the public needs to be educated on the advantages of good governance and participate in promoting it. The public itself bears a large share of responsibility for insisting on honesty and integrity in government and business. The public needs to learn: (a) not to let anybody buy their vote; (b) not to pay bribes themselves; (c) to report incidents of corruption to the authorities; and (d) to teach their children the right values; e.g. that integrity is good and corruption is bad.

Activities Involving Corruption

The following are examples of activities which are likely to be both a breach of the professional body's rules of conduct and a criminal offence. These would be where a member knowingly or recklessly does any of the following, or participates in any activity which involves any of the following:
a) Offering, giving, soliciting or accepting any bribe or improper advantage.
b) Taking part in any dishonest activity in the pre-qualification, tender or nomination process prior
To engagement, including any activity which breaches anti-competition laws.
c) Providing, concealing, or approving work, materials or equipment or services which are not of
The quality and quantity required under contract.

d) Providing false, inaccurate or misleading information.
e) Dishonestly withholding information.
f) Making any false, inaccurate or misleading records, invoices, claims for variations or extensions
Of time or request for payment.
g) Dishonestly refusing to or failing to approve, or delaying in approving, work, materials,
Equipment, services, invoices, claims, applications for variations or extensions of time, or
Requests for payment.
h) Dishonestly refusing to pay, failing to pay, or delaying in paying, sums due.
I) Willfully ignoring any evidence of corruption (in cases where the member ignoring the corruption,
or the member's employer may be directly or indirectly responsible for the corruption).

Disciplinary action

The need for disciplinary action

Corrupt conduct strikes at the heart of professional bodies' regulatory responsibilities; membership of a professional body provides a badge of probity and honesty for those who are members and reassurance for those who engage their members that they may be trusted to behave ethically. It follows that for the public good and for the good of their membership, professional bodies should deal severely with those members who are guilty of corruption.

Disciplinary proceedings

Any member suspected of involvement in corruption should be investigated by the professional body. A member found to have been involved in corruption should be appropriately sanctioned under the professional body's disciplinary proceedings.

Conduct of the proceedings

The disciplinary proceedings should be carried out by the professional body in a fair and reasonable manner, consistent with the requirements of natural justice. In particular, the proceedings should allow the member facing disciplinary action the opportunity to provide the tribunal with all relevant evidence, and to put his/her case to the tribunal.

Standard of proof

The standard of proof required in order for the professional body to impose a penalty should be proportionate to the severity of the proposed penalty. If the possible sanction will be expulsion or suspension from the professional body, or any other sanction that is likely to materially affect the livelihood of the member, the appropriate standard of proof should be "beyond reasonable doubt". However, for a lesser penalty, the professional body's procedures may allow a decision based on "balance of probability". Where there has been a criminal conviction in a properly constituted court of law, the professional body may choose to regard this is as adequate proof of the activity in question without need of further investigation.

Severity of the penalty

The severity of penalty imposed by the professional body should take account of the following factors:

Members convicted of corruption.

 Where a member of a professional body has been convicted of a corrupt act, the penalty imposed by the professional body should correspond to the severity of the offence concerned. In serious cases where there is no mitigation, conviction should normally result in expulsion from membership.

Willfully ignoring evidence of corruption

 The case of senior staff that willfully ignores evidence of corruption in the circumstances described above should be treated as serious. Although such conduct will generally be 'passive', i.e. the member will not have directly participated in, and may not have directly benefited from, the corruption concerned, in law, 'willful ignorance' or 'willful blindness' can, depending on the circumstances, carry the same penalty as an intentional act. It should therefore be treated with corresponding severity.
    Therefore, in the most serious circumstances the senior staff concerned should be expelled from membership. The penalty to be imposed in the case of less serious offences and upon junior staff will depend upon the extent of any mitigation.

Senior managers or senior officers in a company

The more senior the position of the member, the greater the responsibility he/she has to act responsibly and ethically, particularly in view of the influence he/she will have over the conduct of junior staff, especially those who are answerable to him/her. In most cases, unless there are very strong mitigating factors, a senior manager or senior officer involved in a serious case of corruption should be expelled from membership.

Mitigating factors.

A lesser penalty might be appropriate if there are mitigating circumstances. For example, in the case of more junior staff, the severity of the penalty will depend upon such factors as the age and experience of the member, the degree to which the member's participation was active or passive, whether he/she had been subject to coercion or pressure from the peer group in which he/she had been working, or from senior staff. It would also be appropriate to take account of the extent to which clear, well-publicized rules of conduct and appropriate anti-corruption reporting lines existed within the employing organization. Other mitigating circumstances include where the member brought the matter to the attention of the professional body, admitted the circumstances, and/or co-operated with the enquiry.

Defenses:

The member should not normally be disciplined if the sole reason that he/she undertook the corrupt act was to avoid the real risk of death or personal injury to the member or another person.

When to take disciplinary action:

Disciplinary action in relation to corruption should be taken by the professional body as soon as reasonably possible, and whether or not there has been a criminal prosecution or conviction. However, the decision as to when to initiate disciplinary action should take account of intended or existing criminal proceedings, as follows:
a) The types of corruption listed in paragraph 3 are likely to be criminal offences in all countries. Normally, therefore, it would be expected that evidence of corruption by a member would be

referred to the criminal authorities in the relevant country for investigation and, where appropriate, prosecution. In such cases, professional bodies would not normally commence disciplinary action against a member accused of corruption until the investigation or prosecution had been concluded.

b) However, if the professional body has good reason to doubt that the matter will be dealt with effectively by the authorities, or if it appears that criminal proceedings are likely to be unduly delayed or prolonged, it may be appropriate to initiate disciplinary action irrespective of the outcome of the criminal investigation/prosecution.

c) Similarly, if the criminal authorities have decided not to prosecute, or continue an investigation, it would be appropriate for the professional body to initiate disciplinary action if it considered that the evidence was sufficiently strong to show that its member or members had a case to answer. An example would be where the authorities had decided not to proceed for reasons unrelated to
the strength of the evidence of corruption, e.g. citing national security.

Raising Awareness

In some cases, a member may participate in corrupt activity without being aware that the activity may be regarded as unethical, or that it may lead to disciplinary action by the professional body or criminal sanction by the authorities. The professional body should therefore widely publicize its rules prohibiting corrupt activity, explain the conduct which is regarded as corrupt, and outline the likely disciplinary and criminal sanctions.

New Paradigms

In the old paradigm, donor agencies preferred to work almost entirely with government agencies. Governments and donors alike gave little recognition to the private sector, the general public or civil society organizations as important agents for change. Most capacity building focused on "tools and skills" for the executive branch of government with little emphasis on the capacities of the legislative and judicial branches of government or of civil society and the private sector. More attention was given to budgets and activities than to the economic outcomes and impacts that would be achieved by these activities. Results were seldom the focus. And government accountability and transparency were not seen as particularly important. Underlying this new approach is the belief that elected politicians and public sector employees should focus on generating sustainable development results by meeting the needs of the general public and other clients. Politicians and employees should be held accountable individually and collectively for fulfilling government's responsibilities and commitments.

This new strategy can be expressed in the new paradigms shown below:

• Accountability through transparency (access to information)
• Focus on prevention rather than enforcement
• Raise awareness and expectations of civil society
• Focus on results-oriented service to the public
• Develop the capacity of "Pillars of Integrity" to fight corruption

5

CASE STUDY

Corruption Symposium: A Case Study on 'The Chicago Way'

Hundreds of statewide and local residents turned out today for a Symposium on Corruption held in Bensenville, Illinois, just outside of Chicago. Sponsored by Citizens Against Government Waste, the symposium brought together leaders from throughout the state to debate and discusses how to unravel the economic and social cost of corruption in Illinois, provide ideas for effective government reform and restoring voter confidence. The Symposium took place at Fenton Community High School in Bensenville, IL.

Terry Brunner, executive director of the Aviation Integrity Project, said, "This isn't just suburbanites watching and laughing at the most corrupt city in the nation. Instead we're all furious, perceived back-room deals have become the Illinois national past-time. Here at home, jobs and contracts are the heart of corruption. In the classic Chicago sense, jobs and contracts equal campaign contributions and reciprocity, the mother's milk of politics." Panels included: The cost of public corruption in dollars and sense and Moving beyond corruption -- Dissecting the Illinois Machine. Representing the panels were Garrard McClendon of Chicago Land Television, Terry Brunner, executive director of the Aviation Integrity Project, David Morrison of the Illinois Coalition for Political Reform (ICPR), Steve Rhodes of the Beachwood Reporter, Mark LaMet, Medill School of Journalism and Bill Dwyer of the Wednesday Journal Newspapers.

The crowd was larger than expected and the audience peppered the panelists with concerns, ideas and questions. "Of course there is citizen and voter frustration out there with the recent scandals in Springfield and City Hall," said David Morison of the Illinois Coalition for Campaign Finance Reform.

"I applaud the people of Bensenville and surrounding areas who came out today to essentially say corruption is unacceptable." During the panel discussion, O'Hare expansion contracts, corruption and cronyism were mentioned more than once. The O'Hare Modernization Program (OMP) is currently stalled due to lack of funding and disagreements about the design. The emcee for the event was John Geils, Village President of Bensenville who commented, "As a leader and public servant I'm very concerned about the State and City's reputation. To know we are at the pinnacle doesn't make any of us feel better. When it comes to the future of our town and O'Hare Airport, we're all frustrated with the tactics used by the City to promote such a flawed plan. The OMP is a runway to nowhere. It won't help with delays and will cost the taxpayers $20 billion."

Citizens Against Government Waste is a nonpartisan, nonprofit organization dedicated to eliminating waste, fraud, abuse, and mismanagement in government.

6

SUMMARY

Prevention Is the Only Solution to Corruption

It is beyond the scope of law enforcement to contain all of the possible avenues of corruption. The only solution is to improve the system of administration, and make it invincible by adding the strategies of Natural Law described above to prevent the possibility of corruption ever arising. This practical guide is designed first and foremost to assist those responsible for development cooperation projects and programmers that facilitate administrative reform at the national and/or municipal levels. It provides suggestions and practical advice to support those individuals in integrating corruption prevention components into such projects in an appropriate manner. Good governance, based on democratic principles and creating conducive frameworks for economic and social development, is key to poverty reduction. Anti-corruption projects within the broader scope of administrative reform measures aim above all to raise the quality of public administrations, and help enable them discharge their mandate to deliver public goods and services for poverty reduction. The overarching development-policy goal of these components is to help directly improve the life situation of target groups. Reform measures are best positioned at the interface of the administration and its socioinstitutional environment (including the legislative, judiciary, civil society and/or the private sector), and include the creation of effective and independent monitoring mechanisms, as well as incentives to competition, that promote an internal dynamic for reform within the administrations concerned. It is particularly desirable to institutionalize citizen participation in administrative affairs, and/or to involve civil society organisations.The process of building national integrity systems is as important as the content. The following are six final thoughts about the process.

1. Successful reform requires a country to integrate and harmonies all reforms in to a National Reform Program, including: sector reforms, financial reforms, economic reforms, constitutional reforms, civil-service reform, decentralization, army demobilization, privatization, and legal reforms.

2. Reform is a long-term process where attitudes and conduct must be examined and reevaluated for effectiveness at all levels.

3. Successful reformers will have to manage both expectations and change while introducing realistic incentive structures and sanctions.

4. Initially, reform should only tackle areas: (a) that can show credible impact on issues important to key stakeholders; (b) where the return on investment is greatest; (c) that are discrete and where reformers can control implementation, (d) that are within the budget; and(e) that can have some short-term positive impact.

5. Reform is a process of instituting building blocks that must be put in place over a number of years.

6. The process of and commitment to reform must be visibly supported from the top. Essential to curbing corruption is undertaking and maintaining the public's confidence in the State as an institution. It is dependent upon the people's loyalty to its philosophy and policies regarding the development of the society's social, economic, and political welfare. At the heart of successful reform is the State's

These ten country examples are important since they act as regional examples, which are often more relevant and easier to sell to other countries in the same region. All CICP country based activities should be compatible with the other donors' general strategy and an overall larger framework of country reform (CDF) Collaboration between all active donors to put the anti-corruption into an effective overall strategy can only facilitate these efforts. Some models based upon the governance group's prior experiences have been effective, but the strategy must remain adaptable. The model should change as "case law" or best practice experience increases with the final objective being improved effectiveness. Surveys help establish a baseline on which to judge progress.The growing realization that the private and public sectors should be examined supports efforts to develop effective, action-oriented information-gathering procedures. They play an important role in measuring the places where the private sector interacts with the public, such as the case of the TI survey. It is significant to note that surveys used for pure awareness raising and problem identification are going to be less involved and smaller than surveys used for problem description or in the development of a broader reform program. The so-called Service Delivery Surveys (SDSs), done in partnership with CIET International, are in the latter category and are consequently expensive. However, to ensure effectiveness, much of the governance work should be done at the sub-national level. As decentralization becomes a growing priority, more analyses are needed to assess the relative advantages of decentralisation and the process for the efficient delivery of public services.In the light of the diverse range of corrupt actions, and the generic nature of the concept of corruption, it is unlikely that any precise and detailed definition of institutional corruption is possible. Nor is it likely that the field of corrupt actions can be neatly circumscribed by recourse to a set of self-evident criteria. Rather we should content ourselves with the somewhat vague and highly generic definition of institutional corruption provided above; and then proceed in a relatively informal and piecemeal manner to try to identify a range of moral and/or legal offences that are known to contribute under certain conditions to the undermining of morally legitimate institutions. Such offences obviously include bribery, nepotism, and some — but not all — cases of fraud. But under certain circumstances they might also include breaches of confidentiality that compromise investigations, the making of false statements that undermines court proceedings or selection committee processes, selective enforcement of laws or rules by those in authority, and so on and so forth.The wide diversity of corrupt actions has at least two further implications.

Firstly, it implies that acts of institutional corruption as a class display a correspondingly large set of moral deficiencies. Certainly, most corrupt actions will be morally wrong and morally wrong at least in part because they undermine morally legitimate institutions. However, since there are many and diverse offences at the core of corrupt actions, there will also be many and diverse moral deficiencies associated with different forms of corruption. Some acts of corruption will be moral deficient by virtue of involving deception, others by virtue of infringing a moral right to property, still others by virtue of infringing a principle of impartiality, and so on.

Secondly, the wide diversity of corrupt actions implies that there may well need to be a correspondingly wide and diverse range of anti-corruption measures to combat corruption in its different forms, and indeed in its possibly very different contexts.

HIRE AND PROMOTE FOR AN ETHICAL CULTURE

People tend to be most comfortable in organizations where ethical standards are similar to theirs. Those who are opposed to the behavior they see "will migrate out, either by choice or they'll be asked to leave," Cialdini says. Many employees may not know whether the CFO is cooking the books, but they do see and hear about others' behavior.

The problem is magnified when the unethical players are in management. "It becomes very reinforcing as managers select and promote people who are like themselves," Ashforth says. That will leave more people in the organization who think cutting ethical corners is OK.

Adds Wharton's Schweitzer: "If a senior manager has employees pick up his dry cleaning or wash his car or use company money to fund a birthday party, you're setting a tone that's really corrosive throughout the organization."

"There are cultures where you're perceived as dumb if you're not taking a little bit on the side," Hanson says. "There are cultures where you don't tell the customer anything more than what you have to, and there are cultures where you genuinely watch out for the customer's interests."

ENCOURAGE DISSENT

Corruption is less likely if employees feel comfortable speaking up. "Managers need to convey that they want their subordinates to disagree with them, or to speak up when something doesn't feel right," Gruenfeld says.

APPOINT AN ETHICS OFFICER

Have someone who knows both legal and ethical issues and can offer advice to employees when they don't know how to handle a situation. "You need to have people you can actively go to get advice," Ashforth says.

RETHINK GOALS AND REWARDS

A system that bases people's pay solely on how much they sell provides no incentive for behaving responsibly with respect to recruiting, training, and character. "If you tie compensation solely to production, you've lost control—you're no longer a manager," McCoy says.

Schweitzer has found that people with specific goals are more likely to cheat in order to reach them. This is true even when there is no extra compensation for meeting the goal—the psychological benefit is enough to make people stretch the truth. He suggests managers weigh the motivation that goals provide against the potential ethical cost, especially when those goals, such as billable hours, are difficult to monitor. "In some cases, the benefits of motivating with goals and incentives are really worth it," he says. "In other cases, the damage you do to your ethical climate could be far worse than the benefit you get in productivity."

MARGINALIZE MISCONDUCT

Instead of telling employees not to steal from the storeroom because too many pencils have disappeared, try this message, Cialdini says: "'If even one of us does this, it undermines the integrity of the system and the fairness by which we all treat one another.' The key is to marginalize the undesirable conduct, rather than to normalize it."

An ethical culture—one in which honesty is normal and cheating is not—can go a long way toward minimizing corruption. But just as creating it requires balancing competing approaches, so does dealing with offenses when discovered.

"I do think people have to be held accountable for actions," Gruenfeld says, but she adds that punishing wrongdoers

79

should be accompanied by an examination of the organizational structure that contributed to the problem. Simply replacing the people is not enough.

BIBLIOGRAPHY

References

Ades, A. and R. Di Tella, "The New Economics of Corruption: A Survey and Some New Results," *Political Studies*, 45, 1997, 496-515.

Ades, A., Di Tella, R., 1996. The causes and consequences of corruption. *IDS Bulletin 27* (2), 6-10.

Ades, A., Di Tella, R., 1999. Rents, competition and corruption. *American Economic Review, forthcoming.*

Aidt, Toke S., "Economic Analysis of Corruption: A Survey," *Economic Journal*, 113, 2003, F632-F652.

Alvarez, M., Cheibub, J.A., Limongi, F., Przeworski, A., 1996. Classifying political regimes. *Studies in Comparative International Development* 31 (2), 3-36.

Banfield, E.C., 1958. The Moral Basis of a Backward Society, *The Free Press*, New York.

Banfield, E.C., 1979. Corruption as a feature of governmental organization. In: Ekpo, M. (Ed), *Bureaucratic Corruption in Sub-Saharan Africa: Toward a Search for Causes and Consequences.*

Bardhan, P., "Corruption and Development: A Review of Issues," *Journal of Economic Literature*, 35, 1997, 1020-1046.

Barrett, D. (Ed), 1982. World Christian Encyclopedia. *Oxford University Press*, New York.

Barro, R.J., 1997. Determinants of Economic Growth: *A Cross-Country Empirical Study*. MIT Press, Cambridge, MA.

Beck, N. and J.N. Katz, "What to do (and not to do) with Time-Series Cross-Section Data," *American Political Science Review*, 89, 1995, 634-647.

Becker, G.S., "Crime and Punishment: An Economic Approach," *Journal of Political Economy*, 76, 1968, 169-217.

Becker, G.S. and G.J. Stigler, "Law Enforcement, Malfeasance and the Compensation of Enforcers," *Journal of Legal Studies*, 3, 1974, 1-19.

Biles, Roger. *Richard J. Daley: Politics, Race, and the Governing of Chicago*. 1995.

Citizens Against Government Waste (2009) Retrieved May 19, 2009, from http://www.wsj.com

Corruption in local government. (2009, February 17). In *Wikipedia, The Free Encyclopedia*. Retrieved 22:02, May 19, 2009, from http://en.wikipedia.org/w/index.php?title=Corruption_in_local_government&oldid=271406631

Crony capitalism. (2009, March 22). In *Wikipedia, The Free Encyclopedia*. Retrieved 21:57, May 19, 2009, from http://en.wikipedia.org/w/index.php?title=Crony_capitalism&oldid=278850783

EAMON JAVERS & FRED BARBASH (2008, December 9). Why is Illinois so corrupt? *POLITICO*, Retrieved April 23, 2009, from http://www.politico.com web page.

Einhorn, Robin. *Property Rules: Political Economy in Chicago, 1833–1872.* 1991

Eschborn, (2005) *Preventing Corruption in Public Administration at the National and Local Level,* A Practical Guide, Retrieved May 1, 2009, from http://www.gtz.com

Flanagan, Maureen A. *Seeing with Their Hearts: Chicago Women and the Vision of the Good City, 1871–1933.* 2002.

Margaret Steen, (2008, August 15).Stanford Business Magazine, *Preventing Corruption.* Retreived May 18, 2009, from http://www.stanfordstorybank.com

Matt (2008, December 9). Illinois Has Rich History In Corrupt Politicians, *The Right Soup,* Retrieved April 10, 2009, from http://www.rightsoup.mht web page.

Political corruption. (2009, May 15). In *Wikipedia, The Free Encyclopedia.* Retrieved 18:26, May 18, 2009, from http://en.wikipedia.org/w/index.php?title=Political_corruption&oldid=290003278

Political machine. (2009, March 19). In *Wikipedia, The Free Encyclopedia.* Retrieved 18:28, May 18, 2009, from http://en.wikipedia.org/w/index.php?title=Political_machine&oldid=278314077

Robin Hodess (2004, July 1). Political Corruption, *Global Corruption Report,* Retrieved April 25, 2009, from http://www.transparency.org/publications/gcr

The Cost of Corruption, Springfield, IL. *Illinois Campaign for Political Reform,* Campaign Finance and Ethics, Chicago, Illinois.

Treisman, D., "The Causes of Corruption: A Cross-National Study," *Journal of Public Economics*, 76, 2000, 399-457.

University Press of America, Washington, DC. Banks, A.S., 1994. Cross-national time series data archive. *Center for Social Analysis*, SUNY Binghampton, Binghampton, NY.

INDEX

www.ingramcontent.com/pod-product-compliance
Lightning Source LLC
Chambersburg PA
CBHW062048280526
45788CB00003B/1145